DUNK YOUR DONUTS, NOT YOUR CHILDREN

By Linda Bolger

Slipping into the crystal-clear pool, enveloped by the calm of the water, mind and body relaxed, the swimmer slowly releases the cares and worries of the day. This is the image of swimming for millions as a proliferation on public, private and club pools dots the nation.

In keeping with this vogue of swimming as a prime source of recreation, instructions have been given at a very early age – to toddlers and infants. But what about these children? Will they be safe? Will they master the necessary survival skills of swimming? Will parents have "drown proof" children embracing the joys of swimming?

Linda Bolger's book, Dunk You Donuts, Not Your Children, addresses these concerns as well as the controversial forced submersion theory of swimming instruction. The book draws upon her vast experiences as a lifeguard and water safety instructor, teacher, and interested parent of four children.

In this carefully researched study, consideration is given to the child overcoming his or her fear of water through natural, pleasurable water adjustment techniques and activities that can be employed by trained personnel and supportive parents.

The key to water adaptation for the very young is dependent on the realization that the physical, emotional, and social well-being of the child must be paramount.

Mrs. Bolger's book is a thoughtful invitation for water safety instructors, pool managers, physical education teachers, and caring parents to share the pleasures of swimming with the early-age child.

Dunk Your Donuts, Not Your Children
Second Edition

Linda Bolger
with Wanda Bailey

FAST SWIM PUBLICATIONS

St. Johns, Florida

Other Books by the Authors

Linda Bolger

FAST (Flotation Aided Swim Training) Swim Program Instructor Guided Learning Manual and Workbook – Fast Swim Publications (2018 and 2019)

Dunk Your Doughnuts, Not Your Children – Vantage Press (1989)

Wanda Bailey

Divorce Blueprint – Dragon Gem Publishing (2015)

Going Gluten Free – Dragon Gem Publishing (2015)

Weight Loss Back 2 Basics – Dragon Gem Publishing (2015)

Launch Your Divorce Workbook – Dragon Gem Publishing (2017)

Published by FAST Swim Publications
St. Johns, Florida

Dedications

Linda says:

To my parents –
For all their support for all those years,
Jean and Richard Eisenhauer

Wanda says:

To my kids,
Joshua, Jacob, Mairin, Vivian, Caitlin and Connor –
Thanks for letting me teach you swimming,
And all of the other things.
I love you all!

Contents

Acknowledgments

[Original Acknowledgments]

For their patient forbearance: My husband, Michael, and our four young children: Meghan, Russell, Tracy, and William; my in-laws, Marjorie and Russ Bolger; and friends Sharon Tinucci, Sally Newkirk, Leona Tentarelli, Karen and Tom Flynn, Valerie Le Blank, Andrea Pcitti, and Liz Jaworski.

For their medical advice: Dr. Theodore Passon, Dr. Steven Langendorfer, Dr. Nirmala Panda, and Dr. Robert Biondi.

For their editorial and photographical supplements: Elizabeth May, Jan Confer, Laura Oakes, Tom Sundheimer, John Geany, B. J. Jaworski, John Thompson, Tiffany Mills, Robert and Suzanne Henry, Jamie and Keith Wilhelm, Ray Johnson of Olin Mills Studio, and numerous participants involved in my swimming programs.

For their swimming and safety expertise and facility usage: the National YMCA, the American Red Cross, the Voorhees Coliseum, the Jersey Wahoos, and Camden County College.

[Second Edition Acknowledgments]

Alan Korn, J.D. – National Drowning Prevention Alliance Board Member and Executive Director of the Abbey's Hope Charitable Foundation

August Ursin – Florida Department of Health Environmental Health Program Consultant

Dr. Jim Bonner and Cyndi Bonner – Thanks for the reviews and edits

Dr. Tom Griffiths – Aquatic Safety Research Group

Introduction

Across the country infants and toddlers are being introduced to swimming and survival skills. These preschool swimming programs have been praised for promoting water awareness at a young age and providing learning experiences in a new environment. However, the experience should be practical as well as pleasurable for all concerned. Recent research now shows that forced submersions can have negative physiological and psychological effects on children. In fact, the Council for National Cooperation in Aquatics (C.N.C.A.) specifically prohibits forced submersions and advises that no child be considered water-safe or left unsupervised even with extensive swimming and survival skills.

From my own research and personal experience as a swimming instructor for the past twenty years, I have made several observations regarding forced submersion:

1. I found infants and toddlers who were forced under the water on many occasions cried and appeared unhappy after submersion. Several participants cried immediately upon entry into the water even before submersion took place. This attitude appears to be an unhealthy one to instill. On two separate occasions children were found vomiting after swimming lessons where submersion was involved. Infants were found to be holding their breath for one to ten seconds.

2. I randomly interviewed the aquatic instructors and found that many parents removed their children after several lessons that included forced submersion. Classes averaged in size between five to eighteen on the first lesson, and where forced submersion was used the class size dropped. More studies are necessary to test infant and toddler readiness toward forced submersion and total survival swimming lessons.

3. Observations showed that children were crying before entry. I feel that this may indicate that fear has been established. Swimming readiness, as emphasized by

members of the American Academy of Pediatrics and Physicians, such as Spock, is an important factor for successful physical, social, and mental development of a young child.

The following are conclusions based on my survey of swimming instructors and pediatricians:

1. A large percentage of the instructors received their background from varied books and experimental techniques of their own. These various backgrounds breed inconsistencies in programs.
2. Instructors' philosophies ranged from total survival methods to water adjustment programs with and without submersion. The success rate of infants and toddlers varied with each program. No conclusive statement can be made at this time about the relationship of philosophies to success rates.
3. Water intoxication of infants received attention from the Journal of Pediatrics when a five-month-old infant suffered resultant status epilepticus, which is continuous seizures. The infant had swallowed a large amount of water from a swimming pool.
4. While some instructors are trained by the American Red Cross and the YMCA, those instructors use whatever written material is available when teaching infants and toddlers.
5. YMCAs have established guidelines for water enrichment programs for children under the age of three. Force of any kind is not recommended. It was found through the survey results and personal observations by the author that forced submersion was being used at a large percentage of the YMCAs. Despite the fact that the survey results appear contradictory with the YMCA guidelines, each YMCA is known to be autonomous. All but one privately owned pool also used forced submersion.

CNCA guidelines state that trained instructors should conduct swimming programs for children under three to ensure the quality of these programs. Legally, all that is necessary is a lifeguard on duty. The questions then arising from the statement are:

1. Who shall determine what qualifications an instructor should have for these programs?
2. Are these instructors able to delineate instructions for beginners over six versus instruction for beginners under six?
3. Is there a need for uniform instruction pertinent to the unique needs of the under-three swimming student?

I strongly suggest, after completing this study and reading scientific evidence on the detrimental effects of water intoxication, that children should not be forced under the water at any time. Physiologically, studies have proven that forced submersion is dangerous. We do not need to dunk our children as we would dunk our donuts. Total survival techniques should be abandoned until further studies show the long-term psychological effects on children involved these programs. Emphasis should be placed on water adjustment programs, learning through imitation, child readiness, parenting, and communication programs. Most important, proper supervision of a child around or near pools of water should be emphatically enforced. Drowning preventative methods are described to help educate the public to the potential dangers of swimming pools.

This book is not intended to be a scare tactic warning against early age swimming lessons. Rather it is intended to make parents and instructors more aware of the various types of programs available to meet the needs of each individual child in the area of water safety and awareness. Swimming can be an enjoyable as well as a safe lifelong experience.

Chapter I:

Various Philosophies on Teaching Early Age Swimming

INTRODUCTION

The debate over swim instruction centers mainly on when and how to teach a child to swim. Advocates of infant instruction claim various advantages for early age instruction. Some of the advantages described are that the water is a natural environment for the infant due to the nine months of growth in the uterine sac, that early instruction teaches that water is a pleasurable experience before the fear of water can be learned, and that swimming is a healthy exercise that helps build strong bodies and good motor skills. Other advantages described are that children who learn swimming skills at an early age test higher socially, emotionally, and intellectually than do their counterparts, that babies can be taught to become water-safe in seven days, and that a special bonding takes place between a parent and child during swimming instruction.

Opponents argue that swimming is not a natural function for infants, because the umbilical cord is responsible for the breathing process of the fetus, that swimming instruction may instill overconfidence in both the parent and the child, that incontinent infants may pose sanitary problems in pools, and that the infant may suffer various physiological and psychological problems from early age instruction, especially where forceful techniques are used. Other disadvantages cited are that the classes may become a status symbol for parents concerned with achieving early results at any cost and that no valid tests have proven that infants with swimming skills test higher socially, emotionally, or intellectually.

This chapter deals with the various related published literature concerning infant and toddler swimming programs and philosophies. Literature supporting early swim instruction will be presented, and then literature criticizing early swim instruction will be summarized. Major differences between the advocates and critics of early age swim instruction are described.

ADVOCATES

The following are several authors and instructors who advocate various values of swimming at an early age. Different philosophies regarding swimming techniques, breathing styles, and optimum age for instruction are discussed.

Eva Bory

Eva Bory feels that there is no need to wait for swimming instruction until the children are six years of age and that parents should start preparations for swimming with children as young as four months. Bory feels that children can be swimming safely by the age of two. Bory discusses the inconsistent information regarding the age for children to be able to swim. She also states that children automatically hold their breath when under the water, so they will naturally float to the top. The babies are not able to lift their heads above the water to take a breath, and therefore, instructors or parents have to stay close to the children to lift them out when they run out of breath. Bory stipulates that a child is swimming when he can swim in deep water, breathing regularly. In Bory's classes lessons begin at the age of two. In her twelve years of teaching experience, she has seen only two children who could swim freely before the age of two.

Repetition for teaching kicking along with verbal reinforcement is emphasized. Bory advocates letting the child go under the water with emphasis on watching the child carefully to make sure the child is lifted out to inhale properly. Floating should be done for five to ten seconds. If the child is screaming, Bory says not to worry but to repeat the floating procedure.

Lucille Cowle

Lucille Cowle emphasizes that at the age of two a child can be considered "water-safe." Cowle describes how a child can jump in, doggie-paddle, and then turn over on his back. Cowle feels that the learning process should be a happy and rewarding experience for both the parent and the child. Patience, along with praise and encouragement, should be used to help guide the child. Two safety precautions that Cowle feels are important are to have the child wear one special suit when entering the pool and to train the child to enter the pool in one particular spot. Cowle says that the child will realize that he is not supposed to go into the pool without these two elements present.

Concerning child preparation techniques in the water, Cowle feels that the parent or instructor should hold the child securely and never force the child to stay in the water when he is unhappy in any way. Lessons should be short but frequent, because the child's attention span is limited. Methods should not be forceful. Cowle recommends that parents do not attempt to teach their own child. Cowle has found that parents sometimes lose their temper or are too forceful in their methods. Confidence building is done by spending much time playing with toys and having fun. Lessons should start only when the child is happy and very relaxed in the water.

Cowle introduces submersion by teaching rhythmic bobbing using humming techniques. She feels that repetition will teach the child to mimic the instructor. Cowle does not recommend teaching the very young child to blow bubbles because she feels very young children gasp in air and water and may choke. Submersion is done by illustration with the instructor going under and up first and then taking the child under. The parent or instructor moves backward through the water to create a whirlpool movement or pulling movement that pulls the child forward with the parent or instructor. Cowle also feels that the swimming program must be flexible enough to adjust to the needs of all children, because each child is different.

Virginia Hunt Newman

According to Virginia Hunt Newman, swimming gives babies strong, well-coordinated bodies and promotes healthy emotional development. Newman feels that babies are born with a swimming reflex, which they begin to lose around six months of age. Newman continues by stating that the advantages of early age swimming are safety, health, and fun.

Newman believes that an infant who is crying while in the water should be removed from the water. Parents should try to discover the reason for the discomfort. Newman contents that infants may swallow a little water when submerged but burping will make the child feel better. When a child is submerged, Newman feels a reflex action enables him to hold his breath and an involuntary spasm of the glottis and epiglottis will prevent water from entering the windpipe. Newman feels that whether a child is water-safe depends on the child's age. Lessons begun at birth usually require two hundred hours, though a two-year old may learn in fifty hours.

Newman establishes course content for her method of instruction in her book *Teaching an Infant to Swim*. She recommends introducing submersion to teach a baby to paddle from one individual to another, even at two months, and continually emphasize using praise, playing various games, giving the child individual attention, and avoiding the use of forceful techniques.

John Schieffelin

John Schieffelin lists some alarming statistics pertaining to pool drownings. Ten percent of the eight thousand people who drown each year in the United States are under the age of five. The under-five age group accounts for 40 percent of the drownings that occur in swimming pools. Another indicator of the increased hazard is the number of home pools in the United States. The number of home pools has increased dramatically in the post-World War II era. In 1945 there were about one thousand such pools, but by 1966 the number had exploded to more than five hundred thousand. It is estimated that about

fifty thousand additional pools have been constructed every year since then. (There are 10.4 million residential and 309,000 public swimming pools in the United States, according to the Association of Pool & Spa Professionals. [1] Schieffelin states that another hazard frequently leading to drowning occurs when a parent allows the child to play in the pool for a time and then leaves him alone "for a brief moment."

Schieffelin reports on a swimming technique developed by William Knocke in California. Knocke has found that young children are usually unable to swim and breathe at the same time. Knocke has developed a special water survival program for infants and toddlers called "Aquakinetics." The program is designed to teach the child to float on his back until he is rescued.

The water survival method developed by Knocke is taught solely by a trained instructor on a one-to-one basis. Students usually range in age from nine months to five years. Knocke's method is designed to teach the child to turn over on his back and float as an instant reaction to falling into the water. The instructor places the child underwater for a few seconds to see whether he holds hi breath or drinks the water. The child is then placed in the floating position and is given less and less physical support until he can float on his own.

The next phase is called the disorientation phase, during which the child floats alone and is taught to turn over onto his back. In the last phase of the floating method, the child is dropped from the side of the pool into the water. Schieffelin reports that most children bounce right up like corks and float on their backs. On "graduation day" the child is dropped in the water fully clothed and may be left for as long as thirty minutes.

"Aquakinetics" is discussed by Schieffelin as emotionally traumatic. There is much crying and screaming by the youngsters as a result of this technique. The instructor is trained to monitor the child's pulse frequently and to remove the child from the water if the pulse rate becomes too rapid.

---

[1] https://www.thespruce.com/facts-about-pools-spas-swimming-safety-2737127

Instructors also watch for stomach distension from swallowing too much water.

"Aquakinetics" has proven to be effective in real-life drowning situations. Fifteen instances in which a child fell into the water with his clothes on and assumed the floating position have been recorded. Schieffelin feels that infant and toddler survival training programs are not for everyone, but they are proving to be of benefit to children whose life-style places them a high risk for drowning.

Danuto Rylko

Danuto Rylko published a book titled *Watersafe Your Baby in One Week.* Rylko's book was released in 1982 and contains conditioning techniques to teach cues and responses to assist with teaching infant swimming survival skills. Rylko's style is described as a unique approach as skills are taught through exercises accomplished in six consecutive days or approximately three hours.

Rylko sets the stage by discussing elements necessary for the success of her training techniques. Pool temperature should be kept at eighty degrees, and a quiet area should be provided so that the instructor and child may work undisturbed on a one-to-one basis. The infant should not wear a bathing suit or a diaper, to allow freedom of movement, and Rylko feels that the chlorination system will take care of any accidents. The child should not be fed for one to two hours before the lesson, and only a light snack should be given at that time. Holding the child securely, speaking calmly in a low voice, and allowing the baby free kicking motion are techniques that are emphasized.

Rylko's methods are described on a daily basis for a one-week period. During the first lesson the baby is tilted on his side while being moved continually back and forth through the water. A cue is given before the baby is submerged for approximately three to four seconds. Cues are described as a vital preparation for taking the baby under the water.

If the baby doesn't hold hi breath and takins in water, Rylko recommends a hug, a rest, and a burp to cause the water to be coughed up. Lesson one should last ten to fifteen minutes, and its purpose is mainly to help the baby understand being under the water. The keys to the technique are described as smoothness, repetition, and reinforcement. If crying occurs during this lesson, Rylko feels that the parent or instructor should not be alarmed but identify the reason for the crying. Emphasis is placed on never ending a lesson with a crying baby.

The second day of lessons shows the infant accomplishing a solo swim underwater by having the instructor pull the child off the side of the pools. On day three of the lessons, the baby is held facedown at a forty-five-degree angle and pushed into the water toward a helper who catches him after approximately five to six seconds. Flipping is taught so that the baby will turn over onto his back in order to breathe. Repetitions of swimming skills and having the child swim the length of the poolside are described.

On the fifth day the toss is introduced to acquaint the child with the splashing that is involved with an accidental fall. Floating on the back is done for several minutes, and problems such as overarching and over kicking are dealt with.

On the sixth and final day the infant is tossed into the water and encouraged to surface, flip, and float on his own. Repetition and play are again reinforced as Rylko considers the baby water-safe. Rylko assures parents that after using her method an unattended baby who falls into a pool will be able to float on his back until help arrives.

Roy Layton et. al.

Roy Layton e. al. have reported on a group of Soviet doctors and scientists who have developed a three-phase womb-to-wunderkind regimen. The regimen is designed to enable youngsters to reach the highest physical and mental abilities possible. Mothers are carefully selected and then the fetuses are bathed by lasers in the womb. The babies are born in a tank of tepid water and spend almost all of their first ninety-six hours in the tank.

The originator of this method is Professor Igor Charkovsky, who began the practice in the late sixties. More than five hundred babies have been born in this manner. Professor Charkovsky has found that there is a significant difference in the child's early development stages, especially physically. These children have been found to walk earlier and grow faster and were studier, healthier, and stronger. To prove this statement, Dr. Charkovsky has completed an initial study of the first babies born underwater. The children are taller, have better developed lungs and chest muscles, and are far more self-confident than the average child.

Layton describes the process in which the baby is born underwater in an almost completely weightless environment. The birthing process is considered by Charkobsky to be much easier for the mother. After the umbilical cord is tied and the child begins to swim, he instinctively senses where the air supply is and surfaces whenever he needs to breathe. The infants need only a little coaching before they learn to sleep floating on the surface. The babies also learn with little assistance to feed from their mothers or bottles. For four to seven days the children are in the tanks almost continually, then gradually move out over the next two to three weeks. Dr. Charkovsky reports that the water children spend all their playing time in the water playing water fames with one another. Many of these children are no being tested for potential work in space and in high scientific and governmental posts as adults.

CRITICS

Critics of early age swimming techniques are opposed to forceful methods that do not take into consideration the development of the total child. Various philosophies are expressed and critiqued to allow the reader the opportunity to contract the techniques used.

H.T.A. Whiting

In 1970 H.T.A. Whiting published a book titled Teaching the Persistent Non-Swimmer. Whiting writes about considerable changes in attitudes in the qualitative approach toward teaching swimming skills. This approach is due to the awareness of individual differences. Whiting also feels that there is a more tolerant attitude toward the use of artificial aids where previously they might have been frowned on.

Whiting has classified groups of children into two categories. One is a category of individuals who have received previous instruction and are still unable to swim, while the second category includes those who have never received previous instruction. Whiting's book is designed primarily for people in category one, and the major difference between the two groups is described as fear. The physical and psychological factors affecting the non-swimmer become essential for the teacher.

Whiting employs a more enlightened approach to the teaching of the non-swimmer. Greater appreciation is given to the psychological implications of individual differences. The major cause of the inability to swim is fear of water or of the swimming situation itself. Whiting advises never putting the non-swimmer in a position in which he is likely to fall.

Whiting's answer to the suitable techniques of the persistent non-swimmer are as follows:

1) The non-swimmer should be taught in a position that initially does not necessitate the head going under.
2) The non-swimmer should be able to breathe freely with little possibility of taking in water.
3) The non-swimmer should have the benefit of artificial support to enable him to overcome the lack of confidence that he may exhibit.
4) The non-swimmer should be instructed in small groups to instill maximum confidence.

Regarding individual differences, Whiting feels each individual possesses certain abilities and skills, which may help or hinder the person's progress. In terms of physical ability, the performer will differ in initial standards, rate of learning, and final level of attainment.

Other points Whiting has found worth stressing are to be aware of the center of buoyancy and gravity and to teach the back-crawl leg kick to overcome the tendency for the legs to sink. Whiting discusses the mechanics of floating, which are important aspects to be aware of. As greater than that of the water, the body will still sink. If the specific gravity is less than that of water, the body will float with certain of its volume above the water. In order for the body to float horizontally, it is necessary for the center of buoyancy and the center of gravity to be in the same point or vertically one below the other.

Whiting makes suggestions for improving the capacity of the body for horizontal floating. One suggestion would be to raise the center of gravity by placing the arms above the head. In the water the more the arms are raised in line with the body, the more the center of gravity is raised. Shallow breathing and flexing of the wrists so that the hands are clear of the water will prevent over inflation of the lungs to improve floating.

Dr. John Queena

In his book A New Life, Dr. John Queena suggests not forcing a child to go in a pool if he is frightened. Protective measures such as inflatable armbands and life jackets are recommended. Shallow pools are described by Queena as being a potential drowning hazard, and he states precautions should be taken to guard against these hazards. Queena suggests fencing off the area, covering the pool with wire mesh, or allowing the child in the area only with a responsible person.

Marjorie Murphy

Marjorie Murphy, a nationally known aquatics consultant, lecturer, and trainer of instructors, has made strong statements concerning infant swimming lessons. Murphy states that the public, attracted by sensational news articles and television programs showing babies in the water, believes the claims that their children can be safe in backyard pools. Parents believe that their children are drownproofed and that they can enjoy the use of their boats and pools free from concern.

Murphy lists some common concerns to check before entering an infant in a swimming program. These concerns are the evaluation of water chemistry by the local board of health, the quality of the instructor, and the method of teaching to be used.

Murphy states that instructors may range from teenagers to adults who believe that force is the best method. Another type of an instructor is one trained in the "total push" method. The baby is dunked until he is ready to stop screaming and accept the inevitable.

Murphy also states that there are concerns that doctors have, such as what happens when water is forced up a small child's nose. Chronic sinus conditions that can cause severe headaches for a lifetime have been attributed to this type of technique. Murphy suggests waiting until the infant is ready and then taking to a YMCA or some comparable place where the pool meets parental standards and the instructors are well trained.

Thomas Middleton

Thomas Middleton, on behalf of the American Academy of Pediatrics, points out that "the efforts of the parent and swimming instructor are thrust upon the child and often such efforts are accepted grudgingly or not at all." Middleton adds that wide differences in children's mental and physical abilities make effective group instruction almost impossible.

A statement prepared by the Committee on Pediatric Aspects of Physical Fitness, Recreation, and Sport and approved by the Academy's Council on Child and Adolescent Health endorses the three-year-old minimum for swimming lessons. Several other recommendations were made by the committee. A one-to-one ratio of instructor to student is stressed under the age of three in water adjustment programs. Trained instructors should be utilized in well-maintained pools. The committee also recommended that controlled studies be conducted to clarify risks to infants from swimming programs. More adequate supervision is stressed with regard to fencing, parental supervision, and the use of flotation jackets.

David Thomas

Professor David Thomas of New York addresses the subject of water chemistry and preschool swimming. Thomas discusses the effect of the water chemistry on the youngster, and visa versa. Thomas found it very difficult to find information on the effect of the youngster on the water chemistry. Thomas quotes Doug Paton of Ontario, Canada, with regard to water chemistry as saying, "Great care should be taken to ensure the pool water is bacteriologically safe." Paton continues by stating that "running water (warm at that) tends to encourage bowel activity even in adults so we can suspect fecal and urine matter to enter the pool (or diaper) when babies are in swimming." Paton feels a good pool operator should be concerned about the kill time or the oxidation reduction potential of the pool water bactericide.

Paton explains that the turnover rate of the filter or pool should be as rapid as possible. He suggests that a volume of water equal to the volume of the water in the pool pass through filters and be disinfected and buffered every two or three hours at a minimum. An extra-large main drain from removal of fecal matter and up to 100 percent skimming off the top of the pool are also recommended.

Thomas comments on a paper submitted by Dr. Eric Mood regarding swimming pools and bathing places. Mood states that the recirculation system of the general-purpose public pools is generally designed to provide three turnovers in twenty-four hours. Mood points out that chlorine dissipates more rapidly at a higher water temperature. Thomas mentions that even as chemical activity increases, the chlorine will bre more active.

Thomas agrees with Dr. Mood that temperature changes within the ranges encountered in swimming pools will have a negligible effect on water chemistry. Thomas also agrees that both Mood and Paton, that for a satisfactory kill rate for bacteria the free residual chlorine should be maintained at a level of 1.0 to 1.5 ppm. Thomas feels that eye irritation will be less at a 2 ph of 7.8 to 8.0.

Thomas states that urine from a swimming program for babies would have a negligible effect on the pool is maintained at 1.0 to 1.5 ppm, if the turnover rate for a large pool is maintained at six to eight hours, and if the youngsters are in diapers and rubber pants, then the most important question is: "What does the water do to the infant?"

The effect of urine in swimming pool water is twofold: 1) Urine may contain microorganisms capable of causing human disease, and 2) urine contains nitrogenous material, which causes a reaction and then a formation of combined available residual chlorine, which has a low level of disinfecting action.

Dr. Mood also discussed the difficulty in maintaining an effective available residual chlorine level when dealing with warmer water. The growth of microorganisms is also more rapid in warmer water. Mood concludes by stating that it would be wise to build a separate facility designed for teaching children under the age of three. Instruction should be given only if there are cogent reasons for teaching children of that age to swim.

American Academy of Pediatrics

Approved by the American Academy of Pediatrics and directed by Dr. Thomas Flynn of the Committee on Pediatric Aspects of Physical Fitness, Recreation, and Sport, a statement was prepared in 1980. The statement was released to inform the public of the position concerning early age swimming.

The statement emphasizes that no young child, especially those who are of preschool age, should be considered water-safe. The committee feels that infants pose an aesthetic problem due to difficulty in maintaining effective chlorination. The committee also recognizes the popularity of swimming programs for infants but makes the following recommendations:

1. If a parent wishes to enroll his/her infant in a water adjustment and swimming program, the program should be conducted on a one-to-one basis with the parent or another responsible adult. Organized group swimming instruction should be reserved for children more than three years old.
2. Instruction should be carried out by trained instructors in properly maintained pools.

3. Infants with known medical problems should receive clearance from their physicians.
4. Controlled studies clarifying the possible risk to infants and all ages should be carried out as soon as possible.
5. People who own pools should be encouraged to receive cardiopulmonary resuscitative training.
6. Efforts to reduce the number of drownings by children should concentrate on three methods of proven effectiveness: (a) More adequate fencing and other protective measures to exclude infants from pool areas and areas of excavation. (b) The assurance of constant parental or other adult supervision for non-swimmers in swimming areas. (c) The use of flotation jackets for all non-swimmers close to bodies of water or in boats.

American Red Cross

At this time the American Red Cross acknowledges the fact that children younger than six years of age are receiving swimming instruction for water orientation. The Red Cross also recognizes that four-and five-year-old children are capable of learning aquatic motor skills when participating in small groups. Formalized courses for four-and five-year-old children with a ratio of one instructor to approximately five students could be conducted if deemed necessary or advisable by the respective Red Cross chapter. Information is limited with regard to teaching preschoolers, since the major goal of the Red Cross is to provide mass instruction.

These suggestions are given when teaching preschoolers (under six years) and the very young (three years and younger):[2]

1. The water temperature should be 82 to 86 degrees F (27.8 to 30 degrees C) with the air temperature as high as or slightly higher than the water temperature.

---

[2] Courtesy of the American Red Cross

2. The child should be healthy and rested and in a good frame of mind.

3. Instructors and parents should never show impatience or rush progress but should try to keep the children from getting an accidental noseful or mouthful of water.

4. Lessons should be kept short and enjoyable. Instructors should gauge the exact time to coincide with the interest level and the fun factor.

5. On-to-one instruction is recommended when teaching the very young.

6. Parent orientation is important. The parents need to understand their role in and responsibility for supervising the preschooler or the very young child in all aquatic activities.

Regarding flotation supports for preschoolers, the Red Cross feels that support should be restricted to periods of instruction and supervised recreation. When the wearing of artificial supports is allowed, the non-swimmer should be restricted to the shallow area. Supports have a varied risk factor and sometimes provide the individual with a sense of false security.[3]

---

[3] Note that we have been unable to support the claim of a "false sense of security" by the Red Cross with any studies whatsoever.

YMCA Philosophy

With permission of the YMCA and of the USA Aquatic Department, the YMCA infant guidelines have been reprinted here. The introduction describes the intent of the program. The intent of the infant swimming program is to stress the use of the parenting type program for children under the age of three. The emphasis is on exploring the water as a safe, fun environment with no attempt to teach skills until the child is ready to move on his own in that direction. Force of any kind should never be used. Parents should be an integral part of the program for children under the age of three. Programs following these guidelines will be used as models. The YMCA guidelines for children under the age of three are as follows: [4]

1. Any water experience or orientation program requires the in-water participation of a parent, guardian, or other adult who is legally responsible for the child and trusted by the child.

    The program is directed to this parent or adult. The instructor will give any and all guidance to the adult, who must accompany the child in the locker room, pool, and any other area of the Y that is related to the aquatic program. The program offers an opportunity for the parent to spend uninterrupted time, and to experience a closeness or bond, with the child.

    An important aim of this program is to provide socialization opportunities for the parents of small children so that they may share their experiences, make new friends, and learn from other parents.

2. The participating parent or other adult assumes responsibility for monitoring the child's health before, during, and after participation in the program. Children

---

[4] Reprinted from YMCA Parent and Infant Water Enrichment Program and Infant Guidelines with permission of the YMCA of the USA, 101 N. Wacker Drive, Chicago, IL 60606

with known medical problems must receive clearance from their physician before entering the program.

Ideally, a physician's consent should be obtained for even a healthy child. Some physicians agree that children can be exposed to a public swimming pool at a very young age; others do not. Some physicians may inform parents about possible risks to the child; others may not. The instructor should, therefore, fully inform the parent of potential problems that a young child might experience. These problems include ear infections, eye irritation, respiratory infection, and problems related to bacteria against which young children may not be immune.

3. All state and local government laws and regulations applicable to the program setting, including those pertaining to water purity and sanitation, must be carefully followed.

The Y bears the responsibility of keeping the surroundings as clean and comfortable as possible. In areas used by small children, sanitary conditions are of the utmost importance. This includes adhering to all state and local bathing codes and to water purity requirements. Locker rooms must be kep clean, and classes should be scheduled at times when they are in the best condition for small children. Proper facilities are needed for the care of infants such as refrigeration for food, if necessary, and a clean place for diapering and dressing.

4. In order to ensure a minimum loss of body wastes, appropriate clothing should be worn.

Fecal matter in the pool is not only aesthetically unattractive; the bacteria contained therein can be hazardous to small children. Babies must be clothes in garments that will contain such matter. Plastic pants or other "bottoms" that are lightweight and have tight fitting legs are best. Rubber pants and heavy diapers, disposable diapers, and thick training pants tend to hold water and become weighted and soggy. Parents should monitor their child be instructed to remove the child from the water should clothing become soiled. [5]

5. The water temperature should be a minimum of 80 ° F, with a temperature of 85° F recommended. For indoor pools, the air temperature should be a minimum of 3 ° F higher than the water temperature.

Even these recommended temperatures will seem cool to some infants. If the water is warm, children enjoy the experience more. If the child becomes cold and uncomfortable, he or she may develop a dislike for the water. Parents and instructors need to monitor the child closely for signs of chill and have a means of warming the child rapidly. In the case of outdoor pools, water and air temperatures are more difficult to control The general rule is not to hold classes if the weather is too cool. Outdoor air and water temperatures differ drastically at various times of the year indifferent parts of the country. The instructor must be knowledgeable and aware to ensure the child's comfort and safety from cold and heat. Locker room temperatures should be warm enough to keep a small, wet baby from becoming chilled.

6. Forced submersion or dropping the child into the water from a height is strictly prohibited in this program.

Forced submersion of any kind, including pushing or pulling a child under the water or pushing, pulling, or dropping a child off the side of the pool, from a diving board, or anywhere else, is dangerous, even if the child is wearing a flotation device. Furthermore, it is unkind. Dropping a child from a height is unnecessary, serves no reasonable purpose, and could be dangerous. Such treatment could result in trauma to a child's bones and organs, damage to the ears and sinuses, or even psychological damage. Water intoxication might also result. Water intoxication is a rare condition that occurs when the child ingests water to a point where the body's electrolytes are

---

[5] Note at the time of original publication in 1989, disposable swim diapers were not available. These are highly recommended for small children that have not completed toilet training.

disturbed; usually the symptoms do not appear for hours after the child leaves the pool.

7. The words *swimming, drownproofing, waterproofing* and similar terms should not be used when promoting, conducting, or describing programs of this nature because the common meanings of such words are misleading and inaccurate when applied to programs for children under three years of age. Terms such as *water adjustment, water familiarization,* or *water fun* are appropriate and accurate.

Programs that include movement exploration, adjustment, fun, games, and parent-child involvement are appropriate for this age group. The proper use of flotation devices and instruction in water safety practices are important aspects of this program.

8. For participation in the program, the child must achieve head control.

The very young infant cannot hold its head to avoid accidental submersion, and so needs to be constantly supported and watched. For this reason, it is strongly recommended that babies who cannot support their heads at a 90-degree angle (most can at the age of six months, although children develop at different rates) should not be accepted into the program.

9. The maximum in-water class time is limited to 30 minutes per session.

Very young children, those six to eight months, may best enjoy a session of 15 minutes in length. Babies ten to chill easily, and other factors such as the amount of fat a child has also influence the length of time any child may comfortably stay in the water. As a general rule, the length of each session will increase as the parent-child teams learn new skills and activities, but the sessions should not exceed the maximum. In addition, it is always better to end a session early, while everyone is happy, warm, and eager to continue, than to end one too later, when a child is cold or tired.

10. Programs for children under three should be conducted under the immediate direction of certified aquatic personnel with training in parenting and child development as relates to this type of program.

All that may be required legally to conduct a program of this type is to have a lifeguard on duty. However, the philosophy of the Y is to provide quality programs, which can be conducted only by trained personnel. It is important to foster a concern for the child's best interests and to monitor the program for safety and health factors. In order to do a superior and effective job worthy of local YMCA standards, volunteer and paid staff should be trained in the Y Skippers Program and water safety. The better trained the staff is, the better the program will be. The public recognizes and looks for caring, qualified persons to teach this program.

SUMMARY

Teaching styles for teaching infants and toddlers to swim are quite varied. Many instructors and pediatricians feel strongly that children should wait until they are two or three years of age. The American Academy of Pediatrics and the American Red Cross endorse the three-year-old age minimum for swimming lessons (although the Red Cross is featuring an instructor program for infants and toddlers due to be released shortly). The YMCA has established guidelines when teaching infants and toddlers but recognizes the individual Y's autonomy.

At the other extreme are the water survival programs that advocate swimming lessons as soon as possible. Survival training programs have been proven to be of benefit for children whose life-style places them in a high-risk drowning situation. However, some of these programs have been found to be emotionally traumatic and not suitable for everyone.

I strongly recommend that swimming instructors follow the recommendations of the American Red Cross and the

Academy of Pediatrics and the guidelines established by the YMCA when teaching early age swimming skills. Instructors should be aware of potential physiological and psychological problems when introducing forced submersion. Adequate liability insurance should be investigated by the management personnel and the individual instructors. Teaching techniques that have been proven beneficial for a child, emotionally physically, and socially, should be utilized and built upon. Bu9ilding the foundation for a well-rounded, happy, and safe individual while teaching swimming skills would be a priority when structuring swimming programs for young children.

Chapter II

Medical Research Related to Preschool Swimming

Swimming instruction at an early age can cause physiological complications. Some children are simply too young to be sufficiently developed physically to handle water instruction. Hyponatremia or water intoxication, infections, and stress are physical problems that young swimmers may suffer.

Water intoxication due to swimming lessons has received a great deal of attention recently from the medical community. For this reason I have compiled some of the available research on the topic. The research presented will help parents and instructors better understand the serious complications associated with forced submersion.

Hyponatremia results from an excessive intake of free water or SIADH, which is defined as inappropriate secretion of antidiuretic hormone. Water intoxication as described in the UMCA guidelines is a condition that occurs when a child ingests water to a point that the electrolytes are disturbed and the child may go into convulsions or seizures, possibly leading into a comatose state. Following are some examples of children who have suffered hyponatremia and developed seizures as a result of swallowing large amounts of water during swimming lessons.

In one case of infantile water intoxication following a swimming lesson, a healthy ten-month-old boy was treated in an emergency room where it was presumed that he had sustained a near-drowning situation. After the laboratory results, the diagnosis was made of acute water intoxication.

Prior questioning determined that the boy swallowed a large amount of water while frequently "going under" in the process of a forty-five-minute swimming lesson. During the times of submersion, the boy did not choke or show respiratory distress. The instructor noticed that the patient had "swallowed a lot of water." The patient became lethargic and experienced an increase of urging output within one hour after the completion of the lesson. The boy also experienced two short *tonic-clonic* seizures followed by momentary apnea (stoppage of breath_. Fortunately, the patient was discharged after the third day of treatment.

Dr. Howard Bennett discussed that complications suffered by an eleven-month-old infant following a sixty-minute swimming lesson. Thirty minutes after the lesson the child became irritable, lethargic, and disoriented. The child vomited forcefully on the way to the hospital and developed generalized seizures upon arrival in the emergency room. The infant was discharged after four days of treatment, and a follow-up study twelve months later revealed a healthy infant. This infant patient was reported to have swallowed more water than usual during her swimming lesson. Bennett stated that stress associated with ingestion and repeated submersions during her lessons may explain the inappropriate release of antidiuretic hormone.

Dr. Geda of Houston treated a youngster who came near death after swallowing too much water during an infant "swimming course." Six-month-old Jeremy was involved in one of the water baby classes, where he was considered the star of the class because he did not scream or resist. Jeremy's mother was told that the main objective of the class was to waterproof babies. After Jeremy's swimming lesson he appeared tired and napped immediately at home. Jeremy woke up, ate lunch, and then vomited most of his food before going right back to sleep. Jeremy's father found him later in the afternoon blue, almost lifeless, and gasping for breath.

Upon Jeremy's arrival at the hospital, personnel inserted a tube into his throat so that they could force air into his lungs. Geda found that Jeremy had suffered a seizure due to complications of water intoxication. During the lesson he had swallowed a great deal of water, which diluted the sodium content of his blood and threw his entire system off. According to Geda, water intoxication causes an inverse in the pressure within the skull and the two combined caused him to stop breathing and suffer the seizure. The course in which Jeremy was enrolled was not in the YMCA program.

Frequently infants show no distress while swimming. In this next situation a five-month-old infant was taken by her parents into a neighbor's pool on two separate occasions over a four-hour period. At the pool the infant was put into the water and supported on her back. The baby had repeatedly extended her neck and briefly submerged her head. The infant would then bring her head up without coughing, gasping, or choking and did not show any signs of respiratory distress. After being in the pool a second time, the infant appeared tired and unhappy and was removed. The infant was admitted into the hospital with a *three-hour history of continuous seizures.*

The infant was diagnosed as suffering from water intoxication with resultant status epilepticus. This condition was a result of having swallowed a large volume of water while on her back. The hyponatremia was corrected following salt administration and mild fluid restriction. With appropriate treatment the condition was reversible and adequate ventilation was reestablished after the seizures ceased. This case was reported so physicians could be made aware of the risks of infant swimming and provide guidance for parents.

Dr. Barry S. Frank of Berkeley, California, and Dr. Michael Cicero of Castro Valley, California, encountered another infant who, following a swimming lesson, suffered from hypothermia and seizures. They stated: "Perhaps infant swimmers should be supplied with a stomach tube to prevent the ingestion of excessive quantities of swimming pool water."

Another published study deals with forced swimming in rats. Hypothermia, immobility, and the effects of imipramine were demonstrated. When forced to swim in a restricted space, rats became immobile and also showed marked hypothermia. The investigators felt that forced swimming procedures are frequently used to induce experimental stress (e.g. Boreggia et al., 1978). It is possible that the stress may cause a disturbance in thermoregulation. This disturbance was found to be clearly dissociated from the behavior effects of forced swimming.

It could be possible that young children experience stress when forcefully submerged. Adults have experienced panic and overwhelming fear that will impair judgment in swimming situations and will hinder rescue attempts. Possible stress induced by forceful submersion is another reason that children should not be subjected to under-water swimming.

Another hazard is that breathing habits are difficult for a child under two years of age. A child under two years of age lacks the muscular strength and control to lift his head up. Dr. Margaret Thompson had found that infants younger than approximately nine months of age have difficulty maintaining the head above water and lifting the head out of the water due to a lack of coordination rather than a lack of strength. Researched data shows that because a child's reflex mechanism for continuous breathing when submerged is not sufficiently developed, long breath holding may cause instant death. When submersion lasts longer than 5.4 seconds, Holden feels, a baby attempts to breathe under the water. As the child swallows the water, he will become frightened and tense and will not breathe at all. According to Dr. William Haman, a New York pediatrician, "an infant can practice breath control until it kills him."

Other hazards that affect the health of infant participants are the various infections to which the child is susceptible because his immune system is still poorly developed. Both encephalitis and myocarditis are disease viruses found in pools. A study at the Yale School of Medicine published in July/August 1985 concluded that otitis externa was positively associated with the amount of swimming during the preceding week. Swimming in fresh water produced the highest association. Another abstract discussed the fact the 61 percent of seventy child participants in an infant and toddler swim class in Washington State developed Giardia infection while none of the non-swimming playmates tested positive. Sue Makintubee at al. found that swimming should be considered a potential source of shigellosis and other enteric diseases. Swimmers may ingest the small number (ten to one hundred) or organisms necessary to contract the disease perhaps by allowing contaminated water to enter the mouth without knowingly swallowing the water.

For all the physiological complications mentioned, it is important that parents be aware of the potential dangers of programs in which they enlist. Instructors who are knowledgeable of the various physiological complications encountered from forced submersion will use better judgment before dunking a child who may ingest water.

Chapter III

Legal Liability of
Teaching Early Age
Swimming

Liability and responsibility of parents and instructors are areas with which to be greatly concerned when establishing or conducting "Baby Swim" programs. Consideration of the child's emotional, social, and physical growth should be a top priority in establishing a solid foundation for swimming orientation or instruction for younger children. I feel that program directors who do not follow the guidelines established by the National YMCA or Council for National Cooperation in Aquatics (CNCA) may not be fully interested in developing the total child. This chapter discusses the potential problems of which instructors and parents should be aware.

Water intoxication is a relatively new phenomenon in the "aquatics world." Infants and very young children are most prone to this phenomenon, which is usually caused by forced submersion or from being dropped into the water. Instructors of infants enrolled in aquatic activities may be subject to lawsuits, whether or not they are aware of the potential hazards of water intoxication and other water-related medical conditions. A lawsuit may seek to impose liability if one or more of the instructor's students develop medical problems through instructional or orientation programs conducted by that instructor.

According to Marjorie Murphy of the National YMCA, "each YMCA is autonomous" and "local YMCAs do not have to follow these guidelines." Many instructors continue to include dunking in their swimming classes. A recent six-state survey revealed that five out of the twenty-eight YMCAs surveyed allowed infants to be dropped in the water from the starting blocks or diving boards. My survey indicated that of thirty-two instructors polled, thirty used some type of submersion and four used total survival techniques.

John H. Geaney, a practicing lawyer from Moorestown, New Jersey, has analyzed several issues of liability and will address them in the following sequences:

1. Theory of liability for injury or death due to forced submersion
2. Entities or persons potentially liable:
    a. Commercial enterprises
    b. Non-profit corporations or charitable institutions
    c. Parents
    d. Municipalities

THEORY OF LIABILITY FOR INJURY OR DEATH DUE TO FORCED SUBMERSION

Mr. Geaney believes that a situation could arise in which an injured child could bring an action sounding in negligence for damages due to forced submersion. Obviously, each case would depend on its own facets, but in an action against a YMCA or similar entity the plaintiff could rely on the following language contained in paragraph 6 of the YMCA Parent and Infant Water Enrichment Program and Infant Guidelines:

1. Forced submersion or dropping the child into the water from a height is strictly prohibited in this program.

Forced submersion of any kind, including pushing, or pulling a child under the water or pushing, pulling, or dropping a child off the side of the pool from a diving board, or anywhere else, is dangerous, even if the child is wearing a flotation device. Furthermore, it is unkind. Dropping a child from a height is unnecessary, serves no reasonable purpose, and could be dangerous. Such treatment could result in trauma to a child's bones and organs, damage to the ears and sinuses, or even psychological damage. Water intoxication might also result. Water intoxication is a rare condition that occurs when the child ingests water to a point where the body's electrolytes are disturbed; usually the symptoms do not appear for hours after the child leaves the pool.

The above language is explicit in that it enjoins forced submersion without exception until the child is ready to do so on his or her own. Clearly this language could be evidence of negligence in the following situation: an instructor who is aware of these warnings nevertheless ignores them and submerges an infant, causing that infant to develop water intoxication.

In order to illustrate how these guidelines could be used as evidence of negligence, it is useful to analogize to the facts in *Manganello vs. Permastone Inc.*, 291 N.C. 666, 231 SE2nd 687, 90 ALR3d 525 (1977). In this case an action was brought against the operator of a commercial lake swimming facility for injuries sustained by a paying patron when he was struck in the head and neck by another patron who was doing back flips into the water from a third person's shoulders. There were sixteen and seventeen-year-old lifeguards on duty whose attention was reportedly focused mainly on the female patrons and not on the swimmers. Nothing was done to stop the back flipping, and in fact the lifeguards did not assist the injured patron after his injury. The appellate court overturned a directed verdict for the operator of the swimming facility and held that there was sufficient evidence to raise a jury question whether the patron's injury was directly caused by a breach of the operator's duty to prohibit or supervise the activity going on. The court noted that an operator must use ordinary and reasonable care to ensure the safety of patrons and specifically stated that the operator could be liable for injuries from a dangerous condition or activity arising from the acts of third persons if the operator had sufficient notice to enable him to warn against the condition.

The point of interest in *Managanello* is that there was testimony of a YMCA physical education director who stated that it was not accepted practice under YMCA or American Red Cross guidelines to allow swimmers to get on each other's shoulders and do back flips into the water. The court held that this testimony was *some evidence* that dangerous consequences could reasonably be expected to result from this type of activity. Similarly, the YMCA guidelines would present some evidence, if not strong evidence, that dangerous consequences could result from forced submersion of infants. Hence these guidelines, along with other evidence, could form a solid basis for a negligence action. The guidelines make clear that there exists a grave risk of harm in forced submersion:

"Negligence is a matter of risk – that is to say, of recognizable danger of injury. IT has been defined as 'conduct which involves an unreasonably great risk of causing damage,' or, more fully, conduct 'which falls below the standard established by law for the protection of others against unreasonably great risk of harm.' "

~ Prosser, Law of Torts

ENTITIES OR PERSONS POTENTIALLY LIABLE

Having discussed the theory of liability, it is useful to consider to whom liability could attach for injuries to an infant caused by forced submersion.

A. Commercial Enterprises

Liability could attach to the operator(s) of commercial swimming areas where employees engage in forced submersion. This could occur when children receive swimming lessons at such a facility. In order for such liability to attach, the injured child or guardian ad litem would have to show that the danger posed by forced submersion was known by the operation or *should have been known*. The mere fact that the

YMCA has denounced such activity does not mean that commercial operators at this point in time must be found negligent in every situation for forced submersion. The issue is so recent and novel that one might expect some operators of swimming facilities to have no knowledge of the risk involved. Whether the operator should know the risk involved will depend on the facts of each case.

As in the *Manganello* case, the liability of the operator is vicarious; that is to say it is not necessary to show the operator himself or herself acted tortuously with respect to the injured child. IT is enough, as in *Manganello*, to show that the lifeguards or instructors failed to observe guidelines prohibiting forced submersion. That is what is meant by vicarious liability, which is explained by Professor Prosser as follows:

"Once it is determined that the man at work is a servant, the master becomes subject to vicarious liability for his torts. he may, of course, be liable on the basis of any negligence of his own in selecting or dealing with the servant, or for the latter's acts which he has authorized or ratified, upon familiar principles which is in no way his own, extends to any and all tortious conduct of the servant which is within the 'scope of employment.' "

~ Prosser, *Law of Torts*

This is also known as the doctrine of "respondent superior," namely, that the employer or master is liable for the actions of his employees or servants undertaken in the course of their employment (*Di Cosala vs. Kay*, 91 N.J. 15 [1982]; *Klitch vs. Betts*, 89 N.J.L. 348 [E & A 1916]; *Snell vs. Murray*, 117 N.J. Super. 268 [Law Div. 1971], aff'd 121 N.J. Super. [App. Div. 1972]). In *Di Cosala*, supra, the court held that conduct is generally considered to be within the scope of employment if "it is of the kind that the servant is employed to perform, it occurs substantially within the authorized time and space limits, [and] it is of the kind that the actuated, at least in part, by a purpose to serve the master" (Id. At 169, citing *Restatement* (Second of Agency, Section 228 1957).

B. Non-profit Corporations or Charitable Institutions

A very plausible scenario would be one in which a YMCA is sued for damages due to the water intoxication of a patron. Assuming a YMCA swimming instructor engages in forced submersion resulting in water intoxication of the child, there would be a strong basis to sue both the instructor and the YMCA. Since the YMCA guidelines explicitly warn against force of any kind, including submersion, and specifically point out the dangers of water intoxication, notice of the danger can be said to exist and a violation of these guidelines would arguably constitute negligence on the part of the instructor and the YMCA.

This analysis, however, puts the cart before the horse, since the real issue in this situation may turn out to be whether the injured party would not look to the instructor for relief, but to the YMCA, the "deep pocket." This raises the issue of liability of a non-profit corporation or charitable institution. At one time in American history, institutions like the YMCA were virtually immunized from suits for personal injury. Now charitable immunity has been substantially modified in many jurisdictions and wholly erased in others. The law is not uniform from state to state. In New Jersey the relevant provisions is NJSA 2A:53A-7:

"No non-profit corporation, society or association organized exclusively for religious, charitable, educational or hospital purposes shall, except as is hereinafter set forth, be liable to respond in damages to any person who shall suffer damages from the negligence of any agent or servant of such corporation, society or association, where such person is a beneficiary, to whatever degree, of the works of such non-profit corporation, society or association; provided, however, that such immunity from the negligence of such corporation, society or association or of its agent or servant where such person is one unconcerned in and unrelated to and outside of the benefactions of such corporation, society or association; but nothing herein contained shall be deemed to exempt the said agent or servant individually from their liability for any such negligence."

The focus of this statute is on the plaintiff's relationship with the defendant charity. One particularly illustrative case on this point is *Kasten vs. YMCA*, 173 N.J. Super. 1(App. Div. 1980). In *Kasten*, the plaintiff brought an action against the Arrowhead Ski Resort in Marlboro, Monmouth County, New Jersey. The resort was owned by the community YMCA serving upper Monmouth County. Plaintiff claimed her injuries from a downhill fall were caused by "defendant's negligence in renting her skiing equipment, including skis, boots, poles and bindings, which were in a state of disrepair and not properly fitted" (id., at 3).

The YMCA argued that the plaintiff's enjoyment of the ski facility, even though she paid for it, rendered her a beneficiary of the charitable and educational works of the YMCA rather than a person "unconcerned in and unrelated to and outside of the benefactions" of the YMCA, quoting language from NJSA 2A:53A7. For her part the plaintiff argued that as far as she was concerned, the ski resort was the same as any other private facility that charges for rental of equipment and use of the facilities. Furthermore, plaintiff pointed out that she was not and never has been a member of the YMCA.

The court held that plaintiff, as a paying customer and nonmember, who paid more than YMCA members, could maintain an action against the YMCA for her injuries. This result, according to the court, was consistent with the general common law rule that when an otherwise charitable or educational organization engages in commercial activities bearing no substantial and direct relationship to its general purposes, the organization loses the immunity it would customarily enjoy even though the derived profits are used for charitable purposes (id., at 9, citation omitted).

The court in Kasten distinguished that this situation from the facts in Houser vs. YMCA, 91 N.J. Super. 172 (Law. Div. 1966). In that case plaintiff was a resident and a member of the YMCA and as such was entitled to use of various recreational facilities operated by the YMCA. While at a YMCA swimming pool, the plaintiff claimed sustained injuries on the diving board, which he claimed was in defective condition due to the defendant's negligence. The YMCA relied on the fact that NJSA 2A:53A7 was designed to ensure that the funds of non-profit corporations engaged in charitable, education, religious, or hospital purposes would be used to the fullest extent to carry out their good work (id. At 178). The court found that the YMCA was immune from their suit since plaintiff was a member and beneficiary of the YMCA. The mere fact plaintiff was required to pay for membership did not prevent the application of NJSA 2A:53A67 (id. At 176).

In a suit for injury due to water intoxication against a YMCA or similar facility, the threshold question or inquiry must concern the status of the injured party. If he or she is a resident and member of the YMCA entitled to use recreational facilities, it is likely in this jurisdiction under the reasoning of the above cases that the claim will be barred. If the injured party is merely a fee-paying guest and non-member, a different result should be obtained. Should the claim be allowed, as indicated above, there would appear to be a solid basis, using the YMCA guidelines, for a verdict against the YMCA in negligence.

C. Parents

One of the most intriguing aspects of this issue is the question whether the injured infant would have a claim against his or her parents for injuries due to water intoxication. The premise to this question would be a situation in which a child's parents either encourage a swimming instructor to forcibly submerge their child or where the parents themselves forcibly submerge their child, causing injuries due to water intoxication.

Parental immunity is another area of the law that has been undergoing a great deal of change. Several years ago in New Jersey the state supreme court handed down an opinion that substantially clarified the issues. In *Foldi vs. Jefferies*, 93 N.J. 533 (1983), plaintiff Jennifer Foldi, then two and one-half years old, went with her mother to the front yard of their home in Morris Plains, New Jersey. Mrs. Foldi began planting greenery on the side of the house with Jennifer at her side. Jennifer proceeded to wander out of the yard and over to a house two doors away, where a dog bit her in the face. Jennifer by her guardian ad litem filed an action against the dog's owners, who in turn brought a third-party complaint against Jennifer's parents, alleging contributory negligence and seeking indemnification from the Foldis for any judgement against them. Thereafter Jennifer filed an emended complaint adding her parents as defendants.

The court affirmed the holding of the lower court and appellate division in finding that parental immunity barred the infant from bringing a claim against her parents for negligent supervision, it does not protect a parent who has willfully or wantonly failed to watch over his or her child. We think that this holding represents a reasonable compromise between tow legitimate aims, a parent's right to raise, free of judicial interference, his or her child as he or she deems best and a child's right to receive redress for wrongs done to him or her (id., at 547). The distinction between simple negligence in supervision and willful or wanton misconduct is a useful one. It clearly eliminates claims against parents in the kind of situation seen in Fold, supra., i.e., merely allowing a child to wander away from home or failing to pay complete attention to a child in a yard. But the scenario proposed here – where a parent injures his or her child by forced submersion – is not easy to dispose of for the simple reason, that so little is known about water intoxication. The phenomenon has only recently been addressed by medicine. Consequently, at this point a suit against a parent for injury due to water intoxication would probably be barred by parental immunity. This result would be the same whether the action was brought in New Jersey or

California, which does not have parental immunity but employees a "reasonable parent" standard (*Gibson vs. Gibson,* 3 Cal.3d 914,479 p.2d 648, 92 Cal.Rptr. 288 [1971]). Unless the parent knew the risk of forced submersion, it would be difficult to show willful or wanton misconduct, which is defined as follows: "Willful or wanton misconduct signifies something less than an intention to hurt. To establish that condition it is not necessary that the defendant himself recognize his conduct as being extremely dangerous; it is enough that he know of circumstances which would bring home to the realization of the ordinary reasonable man the highly dangerous character of his conduct: (*Foldi,* supra., at 549-550, citing *McLaughlin vs. Rova Farms, Inc.,* 56 N.J. 288, 305-306 [1970]).

Obviously, where it could be shown that the defendant parent knew the risks involved or should have appreciated them in forcibly submerging his child but nevertheless ignored them, the infant would have a very strong argument that parental immunity should not apply, particularly under the New Jersey test, which does not even require recognition of dangerous conduct. As information becomes more widespread about the dangers of forced submersion, parental immunity will no longer be a valid defense in this type of case.

D. Municipalities

Much of what has been said about actions against commercial enterprises and charitable institutions would apply to municipalities where infants are injured due to the actions of employees of a municipality in forcibly submerging the infants. That is to say suits could be brought against a municipality or a commercial enterprise in this type of factual situation. However, one legal hurdle unique to claims against public entities would be the particular state's tort claims act. These acts are designed to restrict or even abolish causes or action against public entities for certain kinds of injuries. Depending on the facts of the case, a state's tort claims act might possibly bar a suit for damages against a public entity.

Another difference between suits against commercial enterprises and those against municipalities involves economics. While a corporation enjoys limited liability in most cases, the liability of a municipality is not, strictly speaking, limited. The general rule is that constitutional or statutory limitations upon municipal or county indebtedness or upon the amount of municipal or county taxation do not apply to obligations sounding in tort. Hence it is not a defense to an action in tort against a municipality or county that a judgment for the person injured by the tort will increase the indebtedness of the municipality beyond the constitutional or statutory limit (*56 AM Jur 2d*, Municipal Corporations, Section 643 1971).

In cases where judgments for personal injury exceed the insurance limitations of the municipality, the residents of that municipality are potentially liable. Their taxes could be increased to satisfy a tort judgment awarded to an infant in the kind of situation we have discussed. For this reason most municipalities carry excess liability policies on top of their general coverage, which, for all practical purposes, solves this problem.

The advocate of infant submersion and its opponents appear to e on a collision course that may ultimately lead to the courts. The outcome is not clear at this point because of the legal issues discussed above and because there are serious social policy issues at stake. Against a well-established American tradition in favor of the rights of parents to raise and educate their children as they see fit, the courts must weigh the rights of the potential innocent victims of forced submersion – the infants themselves.

If there is a trend in this area today, it is clearly toward the recognition of the rights of innocent victims of all types. In the criminal area, legislators are beginning to give victims of crimes a voice in sentencing and in parole. In the area of pornographic literature, novel statutes are being drafted all around the country to protect women and children from the evil effects of pornography. In the personal injury area, states like New Jersey are beginning to recognize the rights of drunk-driving victims to bring an action in certain circumstances against social hosts.

Given this trend, one would expect to see legislation restricting the practice of forced submersion of infants if in fact it is shown that forced submersion poses a definite hazard to the health and safety of infants.

Chapter IV

Social, Emotional, and Physical Development of Infants and Toddlers

In order to touch infants and toddlers effectively in water adjustment programs, the swimming instructor and the parent should be fully aware of various stages of the child's total development. This development includes the social and emotional growth as well as the maturation rate of each child. The development of a positive social and emotional relationship should be a listed objective and priority when teaching young children swimming skills. Psychomotor charts for infants and toddlers should be used as guidelines when developing skills to be used in the water. A child's emotional, social, and physical development should be determined before the appropriateness of swimming lessons is decided. According to Jay Belsky, associate professor of human development at Pennsylvania State University, the classes must meet the needs of the child, not the needs of the parents or instructors.

SOCIAL AND EMOTIONAL DEVELOPMENT

One aspect of social and emotional growth with which to be concerned is the development of trust and its effect on the child's overall development. According to Michael Lamb: "The development of trust requires that: 1) there are predictable associations between at least some infants and adult behaviors; 2) the infant be aware of these associations; and 3) the infant recognize that specific people are consistently responsible for the predictable responses to its behavior." Lamb feels that the recognition of people is an important prerequisite for the development of trust in others.

Lamb states that we can perceive three major phases in the development of social cognition. In the first part of the year, the infant learns the associations of his own behavior and that of the caretaking adults. In the beginning of the second portion, the child has developed expectations that the adults will respond in predictable ways. Finally, in the third part of the year, the child begins to behave intentionally, emitting social bids in order to elicit adult responses.

Lamb's description of the development of social cognition then explains why a child may cry when forcibly submerged. Forced submersion is a new behavior that the infant does not expect from his parent. The child may lose trust in the parent in nd around water situations. Even before entry into the water, I have seen infants voice great displeasure as the parent was approaching the poolside. After speaking to the parent, I found that the opposition was due to earlier submersion during which the child probably inhaled water unwillingly. In so many cases I began to wonder why the instructors were teaching and continuing with submersion when the children were not adjusting to this technique. Through my observation it was obvious that in the programs where submersion was not used, the youngsters enjoyed the lessons, as opposed to the classes where submersion was forced and the children usually objected emotionally by crying.

Children need to trust their swimming instructors, and swimming instructors need to understand the natural wariness of children of strangers in order to be effective teachers. Alan Sroufe of the University of Minnesota Child Development Institute reviewed infants' reactions to strangers. Sroufe assessed the validity of infants' wariness of strangers as a developmental construct. After studying this area, Sroufe concluded that infants typically reacted negatively only when a stranger was intrusive, reaching out for them, touching them, or picking them up. Sroufe also found that if the stranger's approach was delayed or gradual or was accompanied by toys or play, the infant tolerated substantial contact with the person. Strangers with masks were found to be more frightening than strangers without masks; mothers with masks produce positive effects.

I have found myself teaching many children who simply were not willing to learn from a stranger. Forcing a child to take swimming lessons before he is emotionally ready may alienate the child more. My recommendation is not to feel discouraged if a child reacts negatively to the instructor or parent despite all the efforts. No matter what tactics the instructor may use, the child may not react favorably to his lessons, not because of him, but because of the child's fear of strangers. Even though the parent desires swimming lessons, the instructors should suggest that the parent either become involved in the water or wait until the child is older.

On several occasions, I have tested the concept of strangers and the wearing of masks in the pool environment. During the sixth session of an eight-session unit, I had my two assistants (with whom the children were familiar) put on Mickey Mouse masks. Every single child in the class of ten would cling desperately to his parent or guardian, trying to get away. These children ranged in age from ten months to five years. When the parent put the mask on, the child relaxed and enjoyed the charade slightly.

Similarly, several instructors have insisted that wearing of glasses in the pool is distracting to the youngster. I have not found this to be true. If a parent wears glasses on a daily basis and wishes to do so in the pool, I do not object. It is more of a hazard if the parent feels insecure while instructing his child because he is having difficulty seeing. Glasses do become a hindrance when the parent has to demonstrate submersion but should be removed only if the parent wishes.

Principles of play should be followed in developing swimming programs. If toys and play help the infant tolerate strangers, as Sroufe says, then play should be used in developing swimming programs. Frank Caplan in his book, *The Power of Play*, discusses how play develops a child's ego as it builds his willpower. According to Caplan, play and fantasy are vital needs of childhood for which opportunities need to be provided if the child is to be healthy and happy. Play provides contact with others without demanding inappropriate adjustments. Play also promotes the formation of special grouping. The child imitates, symbolizes, and becomes. Play fosters a group life, as it often requires more than one child to reenact home and community life situations. Caplan continues by emphasizing that a child should experience total enjoyment as he learns and practices mastery of his own movements. Having good control of his body is one important way that a child feels good about himself and about life in general.

Suitable toys, presented at just the right time, can play a vital role in reinforcing every healthy infant's innate push toward growth completion. Caplan also stressed that oral gratification is important to physical growth. Psychologists and psychoanalysts have long stressed that the gratification or frustration of this oral need can affect the personality of an infant in a variety of ways. The orally gratified infant is said to be receptive to new ideas and will have a more positive outlook on life.

I have observed many swimming instructors using toys to assist in teaching and swimming skills while in the water. Many infants and toddlers immediately put the toys in their mouths. It is debatable whether the refusal of this oral gratification in the water may later affect the child. Several instructors refuse to use toys, which they feel are too unsanitary. I personally recommend that toys be used to provide additional stimulation, but that parents provide their own floatable toys for their individual child.

Furthermore, understanding the process of change in growth and development through play is described by Linda L. Florey of Los Angeles, California. Florey's paper summarizes studies of play conducted by graduate students in occupational therapy at the University of Southern California. Six principles of play common to most major theorists are described by Florey. These principles are used to set parameters for the studies of play. The principles are as follows:

1. Play is a complex set of behaviors characterized by "fun" and spontaneity.

2. Play is a sensory, neuromuscular, or mental activity or a combination of all three.
3. Play involves repetition of experience, exploration, experimentation, and imitation of one's surroundings.
4. Play proceeds within its own time and space boundaries. This principle refers to a child's interpretation of reality fantasy as contrasted with reality.
5. Play functions as an agent for integrating the internal and the external world. This principle helps the child absorb information from the environment and make some sense of it.
6. Play follows a sequential, developmental progression, which acknowledges quantitative and qualitative changes that occur over time.

In addition, the action component in play is critical to competence. Meyer in 1908 expressed it as follows: "Even in cultivating the instincts of play and pleasure we must aim to make as attractive as possible those games and diversions which require decision and action and carry with them a prompt demand for correction of mistakes and reward for achievement."

The principles of play expressed by Florey et al. are ones that should be adhered to when establishing swimming programs for young children. Proper social, emotional, and physical development of the very young should take priority over obtaining early swimming or survival skills.

Barbara Mann of the University of Illinois discussed strong anxiety exhibited in young children in a presentation to the C.N.C.A. in 1976. Mann described how a child has to want to perform and must be motivated from within himself or from someone to whom he has formed an attachment. This someone is identified as the mother or father. Before the age of twelve- or eighteen-months Mann has found imitation abilities are limited.

Mann relates Erickson's stages of social development to the learning of swimming skills. The trust versus mistrust conflict as described by Mann suggests training the parents of the infant to provide the proper environment to acquire swimming skills. Training the parent is believed to help the child establish a greater trusting base. The second stage of Erickson's model of development is described by Mann as autonomy versus share. Ages eighteen months through four years, the child has been found to move because he makes himself move and motivation is mainly intrinsic.

Erickson's third stage of development is the play age. The child at this stage takes the initiative and becomes very daring. The child may jump in the water, on the parent's head, in the deep end, or anywhere at all. The child will make a splash. Beyond the school age or at approximately the age of seven, Erickson's fourth stage is that of industry versus inferiority. Mann describes this period as being very traumatic for the child who cannot swim. A child's motivation to learn at this stage is hampered because of his inferiority complex.

Mann concludes by emphasizing the importance of child development knowledge for the swimming instructor, knowledge that is more important than establishing a base age at which children should swim.

However, child development cannot be speeded up, as demonstrated by Ames and Chase. In their book, *Don't Push Your Preschooler*, the authors state that there is danger of parents pushing too early. The authors also feel that sometimes the parents are busy thinking about shat they are trying to make the child do and lose the pleasure of enjoying what he is doing. Ames and Chase refer to a baby's teething process. Most parents will feel confident that their child's teeth will come in with no special help from mom and dad. Ames and Chase feel parents should feel equally relaxed about behavior.

The authors have also found through extensive research and government efforts that attempts to speed up various behavior stages have also been unsuccessful. To speed substantially the time of creeping, talking, walking, or handling objects has proven to be practically impossible. Ames and Chase have cited research carried out by Dr. Howard Gesell at the Yale Clinic of Child Development. Dr. Gesell found that even with vast efforts, a parent cannot speed up the appearance and development of basic human behaviors.

Ames and Chase feel strongly that a parent should not push an infant or preschooler in what almost certainly will be a vain attempt to make him smarter or quicker than nature intended. Parents should relax and enjoy the early years with their child and help him do things that are easy and comfortable at his stage of development. Ames and Chase feel parents' pushing may have started with the *Sputnik* era. During this time is was felt that it was crucial not to waste the preschool years and to begin the educational process earlier.

The learning of swimming skills by infants and toddlers cannot be speeded up. Earlier we read Virginia Newman's statement that a newborn requires approximately two hundred hours of lessons and that a two-year-old requires fifty hours. I have found that the average five to six-year-old who has had a good experience in the water will require only ten hours of lessons. This child will be able to perform competently when executing the prone float, crawl with breathing techniques, back float, and even the butterfly stroke.

Despite lack of testing in the area, I did not see any evidence that the children who had early swimming lessons were socially or emotionally superior or inferior to those who had no such lessons.

PHYSICAL DEVELOPMENT

Dr. Margaret Thompson discusses physical development, stating that the earliest motor responses of the neonate and early infancy stages are reflex in origin. The reflexes described by Thompson resemble later voluntary actions such as walking, crawling, climbing, and swimming. Thompson found that research has demonstrated that these reflexive movements are controlled by the spinal cord with no involvement of the higher brain centers.

Thompson feels that the swimming reflex, which is present at birth, disappears at about five months of age. The ability of muscles to support the head and move the arms occurs between four and seven months. Th extent of the command of the neck muscles, arms, and legs and the buoyancy of an infant will determine the degree of success in getting the head above water. Thompson relates accounts from parents and instructors who feel there is a problem for infants younger than nine months of age in maintaining the head above water or in the ability to lift the head out of the water.

Thompson summarizes the sequence of development as going from reflexive and mass generalized movement of the neonate to the appearance of movement pattern generalizations, voluntarily controlled. These generalized patterns are identified as balance, locomotion, and object manipulation. Thompson cites research regarding the retention of skills and the effect stress has on children and adults. Studies show that stress causes regression to earlier though less efficient forms of motor behavior.

Thompson addresses the purpose of swimming programs for infants and preschool children. One viewpoint Thompson describes is that locomotion in the water will build a foundation for later complex skills for the child. This viewpoint deals with motor development without teaching formalized swimming strokes or drownproofing. When teaching this method Thompson feels it is important for the child to be given various opportunities in the water. Experiences described are to have the child move objects through the water or try to kick balls. Forceful techniques are not described by Thompson.

MATURATION RATE

Willingness to learn is described as an important factor when developing an increase in I.Q. Psychological principles of infant development are considered necessary to a baby's success. Several principles mentioned by Painter are: use of the child's senses, use of their bodies, especially their hands, use of language, and the ability to solve problems such as picture comprehension.

Painter feels that an infant's growth takes place in an orderly and uniform sequence because of human maturation of nerves, muscles, and other tissues. No developmental chart can tell exactly when a child will be sitting, crawling, walking, or talking. There may be great developmental differences among healthy normal children, possibly influenced by the kinds of experiences a parent offers his child. However, the child is still limited by nature. Painter states that no baby will sit up without support at twelve weeks but at thirty-six to forty-four weeks most will. Similarly, suggestions are made by Painter for teaching a child various skills.

Security is defined by Painter as a feeling of adequacy. The child who feels adequate will be able to learn from his environment and will be able to give some of himself to it. The child will be able to adjust to the changes of the world and will be able to use his creative ability to solve problems that arise. Painter feels this should be considered a goal of education. According to Painter, learning occurs by trial and error, imitation, natural consequences, and logical consequences. The parent is encouraged to be cheerful, optimistic, and friendly.

All of these principles can be applied when instructing parents to teach their child swimming lead-up skills. One selected guideline suggested by Painter, which I find to be quite appropriate for patents when in a swimming class, is that concerning comparisons. Parents should not compare their child with others. Comparisons are dangerous and the child may feel that his parents have lost faith in him and then consequently the child loses faith in himself. This is especially true in water baby classes.

A child needs to develop trust in others, especially his caretakers. Submersion introduced too soon will cause a child to lose trust, as evidenced by the physical response of crying. Instructors need to understand a child's wariness of strangers. I have found that toys and playful activities help infants and toddlers tolerate strangers better and, therefore, should be used when teaching swimming.

In conclusion, no one should try to accelerate a child's development. Knowledge of a child's physical, social, and emotional growth charts will help an instructor better implement swimming skills. Instructors and parents should also be aware that children develop at different rates. Comparisons should be avoided, as a child may begin to feel inadequate. A positive self-image enhances a child's learning abilities.

Chapter V

Coping with Fear in Early Age Swimming

Fear has an effect on the learning of swimming skills. Ask any adult who cannot swim, and you will usually hear various tales related to fear or panic situations. The emotion of fear will definitely have an impact upon many instructors' classes. Knowledge of this area will help the instructor or parent deal with its effects.

My observations have indicated that infants and toddlers who were forced under the water on many occasions cried and appeared unhappy after submersion. Several participants cried immediately upon entry into the water even before submersion took place. This attitude appears to be an unhealthy one to instill. On two separate occasions children were found vomiting after swimming lessons where submersion was involved. My timed observations also indicated that infants were found to be holding their breath for one to ten seconds or until a parent or instructor lifted them up to breathe.

I randomly interviewed aquatics instructors and found that many parents removed their children after several lessons of forced submersion. Classes averaged between five to eighteen on the first lesson, and when forced submersion was used, the class size dropped. Observations showed that children were crying before entry. I feel this may indicate that fear has been established. More studies are necessary to test toddler and infant readiness for forced submersion and total survival swimming lessons.

In the summer of 1983, a Philadelphia newspaper reporter described a chaotic scene unfolding during an annual "swim to live" program. The reporter described a four-year-old screaming and yelling in opposition to the lessons. The child indicated that she did not want to g under the water and emphatically stated that she did not like it. The child sobbed as she was placed into three feet of water. At this same pool, there were four more obvious examples of crying and anguished children awaiting their turns to learn how to float. The author of the article found that parents rationalized by trying to keep out of sight of their crying children. The parents felt that the swimming lessons would reduce worry concerning their children around aquatic environments.

According to Drs. Ames and Chase, fear should be sympathized with and respected. Supporting the child when he is fearful and not forcing the child to face the things he fears is important for overcoming the fear.

Manual J. Smith discusses fears and their effect on various people. Smith discusses fears and their effect on our surroundings to trigger real fear or panic. Smith also states that fear is the automatic inhibition or blocking of our thinking process. According to Smith, the primitive part of the brain automatically shuts down the action of the thinking cortex at the same time it physically prepares the body for flight. This slowdown of voluntary actions is again a built-in part of our evolutionary heritage that ensures we will not indulge in idle speculation when there is danger to life or limb. To relieve the person of a phobia, Smith discussed behavior therapy.

Johnathan Kellerman states that the vast majority of childhood fears are learned. Kellerman optimistically states that what was once learned can also be unlearned. Handling fears should be done at the individual's own pace. Expressing confidence in the child's ability to master the fear does not mean that we would pressure him to be strong and tough. Emphasis should be placed on the child's natural ability to move at his own speed in dealing with things that frighten him. Kellerman advises not forcing a child to reenter a swimming pool after he has swallowed water. To do so imposes the parent's will upon the child's will.

Kellerman discusses how different things may trigger fears in the water. Such things as being swept under by a big wave or being 'dunked" for an extended period are two examples that may initiate the 'fearful" instinct. Kellerman recommends that anxious youngsters should not be thrown into the pool in an attempt to erase their fears quickly. Kellerman states that it is a myth that such sink or swim tactics are effective. More commonly they serve to increase the youngster's terror.

Most of the adults I have surveyed supported Kellerman's findings. One woman had alarms installed leading into her house, on the gate into the pool, and in the water because of a near-drowning situation that she suffered. She feared for her two-year-old daughter and insisted that the daughter learn to swim. In most cases I recommend that the parent work with the child under the age of three. In this situation, the mother was transmitting her fear of water to the daughter, so I intervened. The daughter at the age of six has acquired a healthy attitude toward the water and has become an excellent swimmer.

Dr. Benjamin Spock has written that between one and two years of age, a child may become frightened of a bath. Spock lists twenty-five different types of early childhood fears. He indicates that perhaps many of them are related to the child's growing powers of imagination, especially around the ages of three or four. These childhood fears undoubtedly have some influence upon learning, including learning to swim. Spock feels that parents should be observant of when these insecurities, apprehensions and fears are most prevalent, if their presence causes the child to withdraw temporarily from the bath, the swimming pool, or the ocean, which formerly the child seemed to enjoy, respect his feelings. Postpone the swimming goals temporarily, and by no means intensify the fear by forcing the activity. Spock recommends that a child never be pulled, screaming, into the ocean or pool. It is true that occasionally a child who is forced in finds that it is fun and loses the fear abruptly, but in most cases Spock finds that it works the opposite way.

Other experts agree with Dr. Spock. According to Virginia Hunt Newman, babies are not afraid of the water, but fear is acquired from a bad experience. Newman feels that if an infant cries while in the water, the parent should take him out and try to find the reason for his crying. Also, Newman states that many young children learn to swim by force, but their experience is so negative that the children may form a permanent dislike of swimming. "Enjoyment of the water is more important than length of time, so don't push or rush your baby into swimming," she advises.

Dr. Igor Charkovsky states that if a baby starts screaming, it is best to switch to a new exercise or stop altogether. Fear of water, which he believes all people naturally possess, need never develop if babies grow accustomed to water at an early age.

H.T.A. Whiting differentiates between fear and anxiety and its relationship to swimming. Whiting states: "Fear is more closely related to an object, idea, or situation, whereas anxiety is of a more diffuse nature." Some people will show outward calm but will be inwardly tense. Whiting explains how some children, once afraid of the water, will do their best to bring about passive avoidance by devious means. Others will suppress their fears and suffer accordingly. The anxiety level differs with individuals and will thus have varying effects of performance.

Whiting suggests that fear of water or swimming situations is a learned phenomenon. Common observations of a young baby in the arms of a confident mother or nurse shows his pleasure rather than fear when in contact with the water. Fear is acquired when the child is handled in various ways in the water. Whiting believes that fear may be acquired from an unpleasant water experience or may be the result of a single traumatic experience. It is primarily important to prevent fear from being acquired in the first place, or the fear may persist through adult hood.

If a fear is acquired, Whiting's normal procedure is either the process of extinction (get rid of) or that of counter-conditioning. In the case of counter-conditioning, an attempt is made to condition another response that is incompatible with the first one. The example was given of an infant had slipped in the bathtub and demonstrated a fear of water after the incident. The counter-conditioning procedure involved attraction toward toys and bodily contact with the other while the child was near the water. This was done to elicit responses that were presumed to be incompatible with anxiety. However, Whiting feels many cases of fear do not have specific therapy and often the fear is not resolved.

It is important that parents and instructors recognize the potential negative effects fear may produce. Youngsters of all ages should not be taught swimming with any type of forceful techniques. Letting the reluctant child observe the swimming lessons by the poolside will enable the child eventually to conquer the most difficult part of his training.

Dr. Howard Bennett et al. of George Washington University address the advantages and disadvantages of swimming instruction for the young. According to Bennett, the advantages listed by preschool swimming instructors of swimming instruction are that instruction may prevent later fear of water and may also decrease the number of drownings in this age group. Opponents of early age instruction argue that infants and toddlers should not be expected to react properly in an emergency and should not be considered water-safe.

Bennett feels that health professionals should recognize that there are variations in infant swimming programs throughout the country. Bennett finds that many local groups offer and teach submersion to young children. Bennett continues by stating there is a lack of standardized guidelines for instructors. Swimming experts feel that children less than two years of age automatically hold their breath when submerged but do swallow water. They swallow more water when repeatedly submerged than when engaged in "water adjustment" programs that do not involve submersion. Dr. Bennett treated a patient who was enrolled in a waterproofing program and stated that repeated submersion of infants may be more dangerous than previously assumed. Bennett et al. advise parents to avoid programs that encourage water submersion and to stop a lesson if the child should swallow unusual amounts of water or exhibit signs of possible hyponatremia.

Dr. Mary Geda of Houston, who treated a baby for seizures and breathing difficulties caused by water intoxication, advises against enrolling infants and babies in water baby programs. Geda feels there is a n element of cruelty in the water baby programs. Babies cannot tell their parents whether they like or do not like going under the water. Geda is content with parents taking their babies into the water provided there is no submersion.

I have found that various procedures and techniques should be avoided because they create unnecessary fear when introducing swimming skills to a young child. Studies and medical journals have cited various hazards related o forced submersion. Psychologists are leery of introducing skills before a child has developed physical, sock, and emotional awareness. Forceful techniques are not necessary and should be eliminated.

Chapter VI

Drowning Prevention

Drowning is acknowledged as the second most common cause of death in people under the age of twenty-four years in a study conducted by Schuman et al. Schuman conducted a study of eleven major hospitals in the state of South Carolina, which revealed a fatality rate of 13 percent among one hundred consecutive near-drownings. It was found that an average of 182 persons drowned each year in South Carolina. Another study completed by Schuman revealed that of 9,420 children in the primary grades, many were unable to swim and 15 percent of those surveyed reported experiencing danger in the water.

Schuman described his study as an iceberg phenomenon. At the tip of the iceberg was the combination of 182 fatalities and the reported 1,400 near-drownings per year. Below the surface was an estimated fourteen hundred persons subjected to submersion but not seen at emergency facilities. The survey showed 15 percent of nine thousand schoolchildren had experienced episodes of a risk of drowning. This represents a high-risk population of 82,600 children in the primary grades at a risk of drowning in a given year.

Nearer the base of the iceberg are South Carolina residents aged fifteen and older. At the base are about 9 million tourists (visitors with lodging) and 28 million travelers (visitors without lodging) who pass through the state and are potentially at risk of drowning.

Analysis of the data revealed that among the African-Americans, and particularly the males, there is a very high risk of drowning at ages fifteen to nineteen. The highest drowning rate occurred for African-American males aged fifteen to nineteen. Overconfidence ranged from 23 percent in black males to a low of 7 percent in white males. (Overconfidence dealt with whether a person could swim and whether he could swim in deep water).

Ability to swim and death by drowning were not consistently related. Swimming accounted for 57.4 percent of the drownings, boating and fishing for 25.5 percent, falls into the water for 12.9 percent, and lack of supervision of children 3.5 percent of the 909 drownings. White males showed the highest swimming ability and also had the highest rate of drowning. African-American females had the lowest rate of swimming ability and shared a very low rate of death by drowning, along with white females.

These findings are relevant to the many instructors who feel that swimming lessons at an early age will help reduce the risk of drowning. Schuman's study did not indicate that this is the case. Schuman recommended that their epidemiological findings provide information for developing more effective emergency care systems, physical education programs for schoolchildren, and orientation for professional medical education. I feel that supervision for small children should be of paramount importance and not the teaching of and learning of survival skills at an early age.

Dr. Pearn et al. studied in 1979 seven cases of children involved in bathtub drownings. In five of the cases reported, the drowned child was left unattended by an older sibling, and all of these victims were twelve months of age or less. The older children were not more than four years of age and had either left the tub or were unable to help the drowning sibling. Pearn et al. described the families as a high-risk group comprised of highly mobile families, single-parent families, and families identified at risk for non-accidental injury. The study also noted that it was not the very young infant who was at risk, but rather the older infant who is able to sit alone and pull himself up. This physical ability sometimes leads the parent to believe the child has enough strength to keep his head out of the water. Pearn believes that no adult should leave a child under the age of three unattended in the tub.

Dr. john Pearn and Dr. James Nixon analyzed a series of sixty-six swimming pool immersion accidents over a five-year period. Pearn summarized his study by stating that 74 percent of the accidents occurred in the family's own backyard. Through visitation, interviews, and precise records, Pearn found out the type of clothes worn, the day, weather and water temperature, details of the rescue, and the type of swimming pool in which the accidents occurred.

Through a statistical study Pearn found that there was a higher mortality rate for the immersion accidents in a neighbor's pool. This was due to the fact that it takes longer to find the missing toddler who has wandered from home and is drowning in a neighbor's pool.

In 76 percent of the accidents it was found that there were no safety fences or barriers. Pearn felt that in only one case was there an adequate fence and gate. Pearn also found that the principle factor determining the survival rate is the immersion period before extraction from the water. Pearn suggests that children who fall into an inadequately fenced pool are at particular risk once they enter the water. The parents in this situation tend to relax vigilance of the young if they imagine (wrongly) that a water hazard is adequately fenced.

Pearn states that some people will say with some vehemence that children will still drown even though adequate fences are built, but he has found no supporting evidence for this view. Pearn has yet to find a fatal childhood swimming pool accident in which an effective fence, one with a self-closing, self-locking gate, was present. An extensive Swedish study of drowning incidents showed that in over three hundred fatal childhood water accidents, an adequate safety barrier was not present in any instance. Pearn feels strongly that safety legislation is important for the safety of children around water hazards. Pearn and Nixon advocate that home swimming pools should be registered, and that the resident owner be required to have a current first-aid certificate.

Pearn concluded by stating that the purchase of swimming pools is widespread, and the threat of pool availability should be recognized. Protective measures should be adopted, or the drowning rate will continue to climb as pools become even more popular.

In another study by Pearn and Nixon, the authors discussed in detail causes of childhood freshwater drownings and near-drowning accidents. Options and priorities were discussed to reduce the incidents of childhood drownings. Some of the factors described were:

1) Environmental factors such as the lack of safety barriers, an ineffective fence or gate, and a tempting object in the water.
2) Parent-related factors such as the lack of supervision, misuse of swimming aids or safety features, child neglect or accidental injury, and unrealistic disciplinary expectations.
3) Factors relating to the child such as inability to swim, illness (e.g., epilepsy), acute injury, and disobedience.

Pearn again states that the absence of an effective safety fence constitutes the single most important cause of immersion accidents. Pearn also found a strong resistance on the part of many parents to erect a safety barrier even after drowning or near-drowning accidents involving their children. In 60 percent of the cases reported, no safety barriers were erected after the immersion accident.

Child factors were measured over the age of five, because Pearn and Nixon found it difficult to establish a uniform opinion on the age at which all children could be expected to swim. In their study they found that approximately one in every five children over the age of five who drowned could not swim.

Pearn found through research that the opinion was divided among those who believed that teaching early age swimming is an effective countermeasure in preventing drowning. Those opposed to this measure believe that panic is often adherent to the drowning situation and that precludes the use of the skills when they are most needed. Pearn stated that there is no published scientific data that exist on the efficiency of teaching children to swim in the twelve-to thirty-five-month-old age group. Pearn continues by recognizing the popularity of the infant swimming and drownproofing programs but feels this role as a general community based preventive strategy is questionable. Pearn states that the early age swimming programs have not been scientifically assessed.

Dr. John Brooks of Rochester, New York, feels that the key elements regarding submersion accidents are prevention and first aid. Brooks stated that physicians should assume a major role along with other groups, such as the American Red Cross, in the education of the public. Brooks recognized certain groups who are at high risk for submersion accidents. They include toddlers near swimming pools, children who are mentally retarded, and adolescents. Brooks stated that while infant swimming programs are offered widely, there is no evidence that they decrease the infant's risk of drowning. Brooks reviewed the statement issued by the American Academy of Pediatrics, which contrasts the pros and cons of infant swimming programs and feels that they discourage the practice of early age instruction.

Much of the information I found documents Dr. Brooks' findings. The following information relates drowning to fatality rates, causes, and prevention. Another study completed by Dietz and Baker regarding drowning, epidemiology, and prevention cited some interesting statistics. The study was done in 1972 in Maryland. All drownings that occurred were reviewed through records obtained at the Office of the Chief Medical Examiner of Maryland.

The authors felt it was important to recognize that many drownings in their study were a result of a combination of several factors. Some factors cited were intoxication and working above water. The presence of a single preventive measure such as a lifeline would have been sufficient to avert death.

Dietz and Baker completed their study in order to determine the population groups most in need of water safety instruction, the prevalence of alcoholic intoxication in drowning deaths, and the possibilities for injury control through environmental modifications.

The frequency of accidental drowning varied with age, the greatest frequency being in the fifteen- to twenty-four age groups. Drowning rates were established and the authors determined that the overall drowning rate for persons of Caucasian descent was 2.3 deaths per 100,000 while for persons of African-American descent the rate was 5.8 per 100,000. Drowning rates were higher for African-Americans in all ages except the youngest. The similarity of drowning rates by race in the youngest ages was associated with the absences of swimming pool deaths in African-American children under the age of nine.

Dietz and Baker felt that it was noteworthy that of the seven children age five or younger who drowned in swimming pools, none was of African-American descent. The authors found that African-Americans in Maryland are far less likely than persons of Caucasian descent to be able to afford a swimming pool or membership in a swim club. This point serves to emphasize a hazard that could be avoided. According to Dietz and Baker, this opinion may not be acceptable to many people.

Statistics in Dietz and Baker's study found that only one drowning was known to have occurred where a lifeguard was on duty. There was an absence of drownings at Maryland's beach resorts, which may be due to the presence of lifeguards. The lifeguards are known to encourage discipline and less hazardous water activities. The lifeguards are also effective in retrieval and resuscitation skills. The importance of training a substantial portion of the population in resuscitation was observed due to the fact that many laypersons are the first people at the scene of an accident or injury.

Concerning pre-immersion, Dietz and Baker feel that prevention should consist mainly of education and training. The current trend seems to be to expand existing programs of swimming instruction at YMCAs, public pools, camps, et cetera, while also establishing new programs through public schools. One of the drownings cited in the study prompted the organization of a "Learn to Swim" program that offers beginning instruction to over five hundred sixth-graders annually. Dietz and Baker feel that such programs will exist primarily where funding is available.

Lack of adult supervision was an important factor in ten of the sixteen drownings in the age group of zero to nine years. This data suggested that educational efforts be directed toward parents living in areas where swimming pools are common. Parents must be informed of the danger of leaving toys in or near a pool, since these may tempt an unsupervised child into the water.

Possibilities for prevention also include early safety instruction for high-risk groups, development of high-visibility swimwear and environmental modifications. With regard to swimwear, in research conducted by Dietz and Baker, 75 percent of the drownings that occurred were witnessed by people old enough to have learned lifesaving and resuscitation techniques. The failure of recovery efforts may be due to the inability of the rescuer to locate the body underwater. Suggestions were made to have clothing manufacturers develop clearly visible swimwear incorporating phosphorescent material. If luminescent materials prove to be impractical, Dietz and Baker suggest the color yellow, similar to scuba equipment, or bright orange, which is used for life jackets. Underwater lighting increases the transparency of a body of water and could be influential in retrieval efforts.

Dr. Peter Scott and Dr. Howard Eigen reviewed literature regarding immersion accidents and compiled various statistics concerning them. Deaths of children zero to two years old were surveyed by Sturner et al. in Dallas County, Texas. During a four-year period, it was found that 45 of 609 deaths were caused by accidental asphyxia events. Twelve patients had drowned and of these, five had fallen into buckets or pails. Pearn and Nixon found that of nineteen bathtub immersion accidents, fourteen occurred when the children were unsupervised. Bathtub immersion victims were found to be between ten and twelve months of age. Swimming pool accidents usually involved older children, 64 percent of whom were between twelve and thirty-six-months of age. The risk period for children involved in bucket drownings was estimated to be from eight to fifteen months of age.

Scott and Eiger felt that it is important that clinicians who care for children should alert parents to the dangers of open pails of water in the home. When treating this form of near-drownings, physicians should take into account the composition of the fluid and its local and systemic toxicity.

Despite many preventive methods, accidents may occur in even the best protected environments. In an emergency situation, it is very important that the pool owner has knowledge of resuscitation techniques.

Drs. Segarra, Redding, and Pawtucket discuss a practical approach to the management of any near-drowning victim. On-the-scene emergency care is emphasized as the most important in determining survival. The ABCs of emergency care are described as: (1) establishing and maintaining an open airway, (2) providing mouth-to-mouth ventilation if the patient is not breathing, and (3) applying cardiac massage if no heartbeat is heard or felt. The American Medical Association and the National Academy of Sciences have recommended that "in children or unusual circumstances, e.g., when the arrest is associated with hypothermia, resuscitation attempts should be continued for longer periods since recovery has been seen even after prolonged periods of unconsciousness."

In addition to immediate physical therapy, it is also important to consider the emotional treatment of the patient and guardian. Thorson stated that in the majority of near-drownings, at least one parent is near the scene of the accident. In those cases where there is a prolonged period of time during which survival is questionable or there is severe neurological damage, an extra burden is placed on the family members. A feeling of guilt about the child and a feeling of negligence with regards to the supervision of the child's activity may be overwhelming. The guilt, anger, and criticism experienced by the person involved in the care of the child may cause him or her to require psychiatric care.

In conclusion, learn-to-swim programs do not make children drownproof. To prevent drownings, safety features such as fences and alarms must be installed. Children must always be supervised by a responsible adult. Toys should not be stored in or near a pool, since they may lure a child into the water. Furthermore, pool owners should know or be required to know resuscitation techniques. This could be down by township registration or licensing. In order to operate a pool, the owners, managers, or residents should be strongly urged to become certified in resuscitation techniques. Drowning accidents involving young children can be prevented with the cooperation of trained and safety-conscious members of the adult community.

Chapter VII

Two Suggested Water Adjustment Programs

NOTE: (May of 2019) The following information is from the 1989 version of this book and is being re-published in the original text. Since then, I have written and published a new program called the FAST (Flotation Aided Swim Training) Swim Training Instructor Guided Learning Manual, which is an expanded version of the following information, and includes a Water Safety Instructor certification process. The main tenet of the FAST Swim Program is the use of United States Coast Guard-approved swim jackets for non-swimmers and weak swimmers unless directly supervised within an arm's length in the water.

The following programs, Water Introduction for Infants and toddlers (W.I.T.) and Water Introduction for Preschoolers (W.I.P.), are designed to help parents adjust their infant, toddler, or preschooler to the water in a non-threatening manner. These adjustment programs have been developed by me to best accommodate the instructor, the parent, and the child and may be used as supplements to other related programs. My personal background includes twenty years of teaching experience (in 1989) with the above-mentioned age groups and thirty years of swimming background. Having the beginning group to the Water Safety Instructor program, I feel highly qualified to recommend the following two programs. Completion of a master's degree in health and physical education aided me in structuring the programs with emphasis on development of the whole child. My degree included writing a thesis for which I surveyed various infant and toddler swimming programs in southern New Jersey. My survey collected information regarding the various instructors' backgrounds, teaching styles, and successful swimming distances (unassisted swimming) among the infants and toddlers.

Using the data collected and my own experiences, I designed the W.I.T. and W.I.P. programs. These specific programs are not intended to teach an infant or toddler to swim, nor to make the child water-safe. Rather, they are used as adult education geared toward teaching young children activities and lead-up games in the water. The time spent is intended to allow the parent and child to enjoy structured recreational time together. Various water stimulation games and exercises are introduced to improve physical, mental, and social skills but are not meant to speed up those processes. References and readings from baby and child development books and charts enabled me to develop these unique swimming programs for infants, toddlers, and preschoolers. The following programs will give the parent, child, and instructor a strong foundation on which to build later swimming skills. When water instruction is handled correctly, the youngster will develop a respect for the water and, most important, will enjoy his water experience.

There are no forced submersions in either of these two programs. Games are utilized that will gradually teach children to submerge themselves. No signs of distress should be exhibited, and there should be no crying babies or children. Occasionally, a child might get fearful toward any water instruction. It will probably take more time to teach the fearful child to swim and to enjoy the water. Most participants must pay for the lessons beforehand, so procedures to follow when a child will not get in the water should be established. My suggestion is to have the parent bring the child to watch the group or individual lessons and then apply the payment once the child becomes involved. This becomes less of a strain on the parent who might feel the lessons are a waste of time and money because the child will not get in the water.

It is important that the instructor be in the water while giving directions. It amazes me to see swimming teachers walking the pool deck with sneakers on. This does not set a good example for the parents or child. The better instructor will be one who is actively involved with his group or individual student.

Slowly these programs will begin to build stronger and better swimmers with positive attitudes. I have seen too many unhappy youngsters taking lessons. Less emphasis should be placed on the ability to swim or become water-safe before the age of six. Safety factors should be introduced at early ages, but the primary responsibility for the child's safety should still lie with the parent or guardian. Life jackets or flotation aids should be used whenever a child is not directly supervised in the water. For example, if a parent is holding one child in the water, another may require a flotation device. However, never leave a child unattended with the device on. It is recommended that parents first check with their pediatrician before participating in any swimming lessons for their infant, toddler, or preschooler. Sometimes a pediatrician will be aware of a program that he feels is detrimental to a child's health.

My water instruction program has been divided into two phases. The fist program is for infants and toddlers aged six months to two years and is called W.I.T. Up to six months the exercises may be done in the bathtub. The second portion of the program, called W.I.P., is designed for preschoolers, aged three-to-five years. W.I.P. is a continuation of stimulation games leading to actual swimming skills. According to Dr. Margaret Thompson, the swimming reflex that is present at birth disappears at about five months of age, but the command of the muscles that support the head and move the arms later occurs at approximately five months. The sequence of development goes from reflexive to mass generalized movement of the neonate to the appearance of movement pattern generalizations voluntarily controlled. Thompson feels these generalizations are sometimes identified as balance, locomotion, and object manipulation. These swimming programs I developed allow the child aged six months the opportunity to manipulate a part of his environment. These programs are different from the formalized teaching of swimming strokes but will build a foundation for later complex skills.

Parents should be given guidelines (YMCA or Red Cross) to which instruction should adhere. The instructor can teach five different skill levels with five different youngsters in the same class. Parents must be aware of this. One child may still need to jump into the parent's outstretched arms while the next child may be ready to have the parent move farther away but still catch him. Instructors should advise parents accordingly, never allowing a parent to move too far away when the child expresses fear or displeasure. Sometimes this is difficult, because some parents want their child to do just as well as the next child. The instructor should tell the parent to relax and to move closer and explain that it is more important to develop confidence and self-esteem than to force the child beyond his personal limits. Forcing a child in the water may create psychological trauma.

The program begins with a handout given to parents during registration. The purpose of the handout is to eliminate a lengthy introduction during the first session, especially when parents are holding infants or toddlers. Instructors should include their credentials in the handout. A brief review of the handout is given during the first lesson. (See appendix.)

The first several sessions are adjustment and introductory phases. It is important for the instructor to know that he might be coordinating children who have already gone through the program with those who are new participants. Repetition is fundamental to a proper background for swimming skills. Plenty of activities are given to utilize thirty minutes of instruction time. This time may be shortened considering the child and environmental conditions. An optimistic and friendly attitude is important as well as continual encouragement to have the child try new skills. This encouragement will help the child feel good about himself and optimistic about his ability. Keep the child interested in learning and willing to work. Little surprises like stars, stickers, pictures, or balloons will keep the child looking forward to the next lesson.

These activities are adaptable to any type of pool as long as there is a shallow area (no more than four feet deep). Pools that have a varied use must maintain a consistent temperature to accommodate a wide range of members. A higher temperature is not always conducive to lap swimmers or swim teams. Pools that can maintain a temperature of eighty to eighty-four degrees will be able to keep the majority of members and swimmers satisfied. If the water temperature is below a comfortable or standard level, the instructor should shorten the lesson and allow the participant a makeup lesson. This may be time-consuming for the instructor, but the positive public relations will pay off.

Infants and toddler participants should wear swim diapers, it will help prevent foreign materials from entering the pool's water (2019 update from original recommendation). I disagree with the instructors who have their infants and toddlers stripped to the bare essentials and insist that the pool's filtration system will take care of everything. This may be suitable for private or backyard pools, but where the pools are frequented by a varied population, the members should be given consideration in this matter and accidents should be prevented. The ultimate environment is to have a separate pool for infant and toddler classes. If separation is not possible, safeguards can be provided by alerting the general members.

Finally, water chemistry should be tested immediately following these classes, for the optimal safety of all swimmers.

As each activity is introduced, the instructor should explain that the child is being taught to mimic or imitate his behavior. The child will do each skill only when he is ready. Each exercise should be done for thirty seconds to one minute. As the lessons progress, the length of time may be increased, due to a longer attention span.

When teaching in a group situation, the instructor should either demonstrate with a doll or show the parents with a child what he expects them to accomplish. Proper positioning and handling will develop confidence and enjoyment for both the child and parent.

These activities are designed to aid the qualified and certified instructor in guiding the parents and child through water orientation. Parents may utilize these skills by themselves as long as they do not subject their child to any physical hazards or mental anguish. However, water instruction should be taught by a certified person. An instructor may be a certified lifeguard or Water Safety Instructor knowledgeable in water introduction techniques or a certified YMCA instructor.

NOTE: There are currently many nationally recognized Water Safety Instructor certification programs available, including the FAST Swim Program. Parents are encouraged to seek instruction and certification in a nationally recognized program before instructing their children.

PART I: WATER INTRODUCTION FOR INFANTS AND TODDLERS (W.I.T.) (AGE SIX MONTHS TO TWO YEARS)

Phase I. Activities from Edge of Pool

Parents sit on the pool's edge, with their infants or toddlers placed between the parents' legs. The instructor briefly discusses what he plans to accomplish for the lesson. The instructor should be positioned in the water facing the group.

1. Flutter Kick: Before entering the water, the parent holds the child's knees and practices the flutter kick. After a brief practice, ask the child to try kicking by himself.
2. Sprinkling: While the parent is still sitting on poolside, have him sprinkle water on the child's shoulders, legs, and stomach.
3. Arm movement: Since the child's back is still supported by the parent, the parent demonstrates the doggie paddle arm movement by hand support and directing the child. At this time instructors explain again that each child will progress at his own pace and that the parent's patience will bring about quicker learning.

[

4. Pool entry: When the parents and children enter the water, there are several methods that may be employed. In some pools, steps are provided that enable the parent to walk in holding the child. Other pools provide entry by a ladder. In some cases the baby is handed to the instructor, who is already in the water, and then the baby is handed back after the parent is in the water. It is safer to hand the child to hand the child to another adult and enter the pool, by the ladder without having to hold a child. Some pools are shallow enough to allow the parent and child to slide in together from the wall. The parents may want to get in first while holding the child and then bringing the child in. Instructors may assist the parent with this method. Whatever method is used for entry, safety factors are emphasized for both the parent and child.

Phase 2. Activities in the Pool

Once the participants are in the water, I have found that having the parents and children in a circle or horseshoe works best. Circle movement may be done with the instructor in the middle or with the instructor included in the circle giving directions.

1. Water acclimation
    a. First the parent bends his knees and bounces gently up and down to orient the child to the water and its temperature.
    b. The parent holds the child securely under his arm and sways the child from side to side. While swaying, he gradually brings the child's ears and head closer to the water until both sides of the head are wet. The parents are warned not to allow water to get into the child's mouth and to encourage the child through this exercise to alleviate fear.

2. Kicking
   a. Assisted kicking: The parent lays the child on his stomach with his head resting on the parent's shoulder. The parent extends his arms under the child's body to his knees. They practice a straight leg kick, moving in a circle with the parent explaining to the child that he is kicking.
   b. Unassisted kicking: Occasionally, the parent lets go of the knees to see if the child can execute the skill himself. As the lessons progress, the child will be able to do this skill as the parent gives the verbal cue kick. The instructor explains to the parent not to get discouraged if the child does not kick on cue.
   c. Support back kicking: The parent reverses the position of the child and places him on his back. The parent extends his arms under the child's body and practices the kick.

d. Swaying back kicking: In the same position the parent supports the upper arms from behind and the child sways right to left while encouraging the child to kick by himself. Allowing the child to see the parent's face is important and should be emphasized.

e. Balloon kick: As lessons progress, the parent ties balloons on the child's ankles to stimulate kicking action, considering safety factors and using loose binding materials around the ankles.

3. Transition stage

A transition stage where the child is put on his stomach and then his back is repeated several times. When doing this exercise, make sure the child's face or mouth does not go under the water. This exercise will slowly help adjust the child to the changing positions.

4. Blowing and Submerging

a. Pulling child and blowing in his face: The parent walks backwards through the water while holding the child securely. The parent pulls the child toward him and begins to blow in his face. This will tickle and most children will laugh and smile.

b. Parent submerging and blowing bubbles: After blowing into the child's face, the parent begins to submerge himself but not the child. It is important for the parent to show the child how much fun going under the water can be. If parents do not like to go under the water, they may blow bubbles with their mouths or use straws. In the beginning many young children may not pay attention as the parent disappears and reappears from under the water. As this process is repeated, the child will begin to enjoy the game because it is nonthreatening to him. Children will take pride in the fact that they can imitate their moms or dads. Only allow the children to put his face in the water when he is physically able to demonstrate the skill of voluntary exhaling or blowing bubbles. This should be done above the water before it is tried under the water. The reinforcement of positive and nonthreatening submersion should be done at the beginning and end of the session. The instructor may wish to continue rotating in a circle or to change the formation. At this time I recommend changing the class formation to a straight line against the wall.

c. Moving up and down in horizontal position: While walking backward, teach the parent to pull the child up and down while in a horizontal position. The head will remain above the water. As the child's chin touches the water, direct the parent to blow in the child's face to demonstrate exhalation. Repeat and pull across the pool On the next repetition the instructor tells the parent to go under the water on the cue "down" while the child is held above the water. If a parent is uncomfortable going under the water, direct him simply to put his chin near the water and demonstrate exhaling.

5. Moving arms

The parent leans against the wall in the water while balancing on one foot. The child is placed on the parent's bent knee and works the child's arm in a doggie-paddle motion. The parent releases his arms to see whether the child can do it himself. Stimulate arm motion by throwing toys and having the child retrieve them.

6. Reentry into the pool
   a. Pulling the child in: In the line formation, the parent places the child on the pool's edge and then pulls the child in by holding him securely under the arms, never pulling him by his hands, as this restricts movement. Pulling the child in is repeated several times.
   b. Pulling the child in and blowing in his face: Next the parent adds blowing in the child's face as he is pulled in.
   c. Pulling child in while parent submerges: The last step in this exercise is to pull the child in and have the parent blow bubbles or submerge as the child enters the water. Do not pull the child under.

7. Grabbing the wall
   a. Back pulling to front position: The parents, in their line formation, pull their children away from the wall on their back approximately six feet. While supporting the child's underarms, the parent then reverses the position and tells the child to grab the wall. This is a beginning of early safety training.
   b. Holding the wall momentarily: When the child has learned to successfully grab and hold the wall, the parent lets go of the child momentarily. As the child's strength and endurance increase, the parent determines whether he can hold on for a count of ten. This exercise will help build the child's upper body strength.

c. Grabbing a safety device: Extend this exercise to include grabbing a pole, towel, or safety line. Repetition of this exercise will help teach a child to react in an emergency situation.

8. Leaving the pool
    a. Climbing out: If the child appears strong enough, he is allowed to climb out himself. The parent assists the child and watches his chin and face so he does not fall forward. The child is not permitted to walk or crawl away from the parent's reach.*[6]
    b. Jumping back in: Once out of the water, the child jumps back to the parent and the process is repeated. As confidence builds, teach the child to free-jump into the water. Have the child bend his knees and jump away from the wall. Instruct the parent to catch the child before the child's head submerges.

9. Balancing
    a. Rotating in a horizontal position: Show the parent how to hold the child under the chest and stomach and rotate the child in a circle. Have the children extend their arms and kick their feet. This helps teach balancing position for the doggie paddle.
    b. Changing directions: Reverse directions by going frontward and backward while the child remains on his stomach.

10. Kickboard introduction
    a. Positioning: Instruct the parent to hold the child securely from the side and allow for the child to balance and explore on the kickboard.
    b. Blowing bubbles: Have the parent demonstrate blowing bubbles while the child is on the kickboard.

---

[6] Be aware of the various pool edges and gutters. The instructor in charge should inform the parents and in turn the child of any potential hazards.

11. Doggie paddle
    a. Supporting with two hands: Hold the child with two hands extended under the stomach while he doggie paddles and kicks.
    b. Support with one hand and continue to emphasize doggie paddle and kick.
    c. Switching hands: The child continues doggie-paddling, and the parent switches supporting hands. For the infants, switch hands approximately every five seconds to allow less support. If necessary, support them on a side with the free hand. Have the toddlers tell you when to switch. The children love this exercise as they gradually begin to do more doggie-paddling on their own.

Any one of the ten activities from which the class benefitted that day or in which they showed improvement can be repeated. Repetition and positive reinforcement of these exercises will help build a good foundation for later swimming skills.

After the instructional portion of each lesson, one or more of the following games may be played for one to five minutes. Instructors and parents should both observe the attention span of the children and progress accordingly.

Water Orientation Games

Game 1

Each parent obtains floatable toys from the toy basket provided, or parents may bring their own toys if they wish. The group is now working on eye and hand coordination by having the children grasp and release objects in the water. After the child has grasped the object, the parent gently removes it, throws I a short distance away, and then guides the child to the object and allows him to retrieve it. Both arms of the child are exercised. The child is offered objects out of his reach so that he may practice reaching, strengthening, and grasping skills. The child is offered a second and third object to help him understand the need for releasing one object to retrieve the other. This will help develop motor and mental skills.

Game 2

As the lessons progress, the parent holds the object or brightly colored toy under the water. The toy is submerged approximately two to four inches, and the child is allowed to reach for it.

Game 3

Plastic play mirrors are a good resource for instruction and training. The child learns how to blow bubbles while he is watching himself perform this feat in the mirror.

Game 4

The child and parent blow Ping-Pong balls or other small floatable object across the water

Game 5

Children love puppet shows, and plastic or rubber puppets can be used in the water. The puppet can pop up from under the water. Little games can be played such as "Snoopy is going to get your nose" or "Cookie Monster is going to get your head wet."

Game 6

Bells or balloons are tied on the child's ankles to promote kicking motion.

Game 7

Parents play pat-a-cake with their children's feet while supporting their backs.

Game 8

Parents play and swing rock-a-bye baby, cradling their children securely.

Game 9

Parents show their children how to use cups and pour water on a doll's head. The child is asked to try it. When physically and mentally able, the child pours water on the parent's head, and then the parent asks the child if he may pour water on his head. For infants, parents may try it and watch for a positive reaction. If the child seems discontent, then the parent should stop. Colored sponges, possibly cut into interesting shapes, can aid the parent and instructor with getting the child's head wet.

Game 10

The children are shown how to blow bubbles. Parents are given bottles of bubbles and told to create a bubbly atmosphere.

Game 11

The parents build blocks and then blow them over. The blocks may be put either on kickboards, a floating island, or the pool's edge.

Game 12

An activity rope is stimulating for infants and toddlers and will help build physical, mental, and social skills. The rope requires approximately twenty minutes' preparation time and must be hung when there will be no interference from other swimmers. Once hung, the rope provides varied activities for the infant and toddler-age group, which will prove to be quite enjoyable.

A clothesline is hung across the area where the instruction is given and extended approximately four feet above the water level. Plastic curtain hooks are snapped on to hold whatever will interest children. The parent may hold the child from behind, under the arms, at the waist, or from the upper leg, allowing the child to reach, grab, pull, and play with the many toys.

Some of the objects I have used to stimulate while in the water are.

1. Dangling and brightly colored toys
2. Music or wind chimes
3. Spoons dangling from strings, attached to one hook
4. Pop beads that pull apart
5. Pull toys that are activated when pulled
6. Toys that react or respond when buttons are pushed or wheels turned
7. Pegboards

8. Squeezable toys
9. Buckets that, when pulled, pour water out (practice
    taking a shower together)
10. Bells or rattles
11. Punching bags

The list can go on or toys improved as the instructor discovers which toys the children are more familiar with. Toys that are small enough to be put in a child's mouth should not be used.

PART II. WATER INTRODUCTION FOR PRESCHOOLERS (W.I.P.) (AGE THREE TO FIVE)

I begin the preschool age group similarly to the infant and toddler level. The W.I.T. program is fine for the first several lessons for preschoolers, but more activities must be added to stimulate and maintain interest. Fear is sometimes evident in this age group, and various ability levels may be present. Commander Wilbert E. Longfellow, the founder of the Red Cross, used the motto "Keep the Fun in Fundamentals" and applied it for years when teaching swimming. This motto, used with stunts recommended and organized in a chapter of the *Red Cross Swimming and Aquatics Safety Book*, has proven to be very beneficial to me. Over the years I have organized a specific program designed especially for the preschoolers, incorporating several of the Red Cross games for instruction. I strongly recommend that all swimming instructors obtain a copy of the *Red Cross Swimming and Aquatics Safety Book*[7].

I have found that when I use the wading pool as opposed to the shallow end of the pool, the children progress very quickly. Wading pools are usually available during warmer weather in outdoor facilities and should always be utilized to the fullest extent. I explain to the parents, who usually have registered for eight sessions, that I will usually spend the first three or four sessions in the wading pool. The last four sessions will be spent in the shallow area of the large pool, at which time I require parents or volunteers to assist with the instruction. This method provides one-on-one instruction for the child. Sometimes it is necessary for a child to repeat this level of instruction several times before moving to the Red Cross beginner skills. The extra time spent in the wading pool is sometimes just what the child needs to develop more

---

[7] Second Edition recommendation – I have published a new program called the FAST (Flotation Aided Swim Training) Swim Program Instructor Guided Learning Manual and prefer that my instructors use this manual currently.

confidence in the water. In some wading pools, be aware of a difference in water depth. I would recommend that all movement be done across the same depth of water.

Remind participants that some skills may be redundant from the W.I.T. program. Instruction will occur in both the shallow area of the pool and the wading pool. Instruction for this group in the shallow area of the pool has been divided into four phases. They are land drill exercises, activities from the edge of the pool, activities in the pool, and safety techniques. Always teach the progressive steps for the new participants.

SHALLOW AREA POOL INSTRUCTION FOR PRESCHOOLERS

Phase 1. Land Drill Exercises

At the beginning of each swimming session, land drills are practiced before entry into the water. These activities will help relieve any anxieties the children might have about the lessons and will build confidence. These drills include blowing bubbles, practicing crawl stroke arms, and sitting down and flutter kicking. The parents assist if necessary.

The group is organized so the children are facing the instructor and the adults are standing directly behind their children. The group faces the pool or away from it, whichever has the least distractions, while instructions are given. A nice icebreaker is to tell the child to huff and puff and blow the parent or instructor into the water. The parent should climb into the water rather than fall in. Once the parent is in the water, activities may continue from there.

Phase 2. Activities from the Edge of the Pool

The parent enters the shallow area of the pool and faces the child, who is now sitting on the pool's edge. The child is in a sitting position with legs dangling over the edge. The parent and child then try the following activities:

1. The child practices the straight leg flutter kick above the water and then in the water.
2. The child blows water out of the adult's cupped hands.
3. The parent fills his cupped hands with water and splashes his own face.
4. The child splashes the adult's face by pushing the adult's hands.
5. The child uses cups to pour water on his parent's head.
6. The parent pours water on the child's head if the child agrees.
7. The parent and child splash water up in the air to make is rain.

Phase 3. Activities in the Pool

The group is organized in the water in a formation suitable for instruction and practice (straight line or circle).

The following activities are practiced and demonstrated by the instructor first, when possible, and each activity is kept brief but fun.

1. The child practices the straight leg kick (parent supports under the stomach).
2. The adult blows in the child's face, and then the child imitates the parent. The adult and child are face to face, with the adult holding the child under the arm. Have the child blow and object or towy forward in this position.
3. The child blows bubbles.
4. The adult bobs up and down to demonstrate submersion while holding the child above water.
5. The child combines the kick and blowing bubbles.
6. The child practices the front float and the back float with the parent pulling the child through the water by holding the child under the armpit.
7. The child is held under the chest and stomach while in a prone float and whirled in a circle in one direction and then in the opposite direction.

8. The child is held under the arms as the parent sways the child from side to side.
9. The child is held under the chest with two hands in a front float, then with one hand, and then with the other hand. The child tells the adult when to switch hands. As lessons progress, the child is released momentarily and caught immediately.
10. The child practices back floating to front floating and grabbing the wall. Pull the child backward and reverse to a prone float position, moving to the wall. Never let the child's head go under until he is ready. Have the child grab the wall and hold on to a count of ten. Repeat this drill several times.
11. The child stands on the edge of the pool and then jumps into the parent's outstretched arms. As the child's confidence increases, the parent moves a step away. Soon the child will let the adult keep moving farther away. It may be necessary to teach the free jump before this activity is done.
12. The child is held from behind under the arms while the parent (directed by the instructor) teaches the child the arm and leg movements for treading water.
13. The lesson ends with races or tag football. Both parent and child will enjoy this type of culminating activity.

Phase 4. Safety Techniques

1. In the water
   a. The child is introduced to the buddy system by having the child show a friend what he has learned that day in the water.
   b. The instructor emphasizes and practices safety techniques. He shows the child and the techniques of a non-swimming safety rescue utilizing reaching with towels, poles, arms, or legs. The child is taught never to let go of the wall and to yell for assistance or help. The instructor demonstrates pulling someone to the side or to safety and lifting his head above water.

c. It is just as important to teach the child how to be a victim. Use a ring buoy or flotation device to demonstrate use.

2. Out of the water
    a. The instructor demonstrates the use of the pool's ring buoys and safety devices.
    b. The instructor introduces resuscitation and cardiopulmonary resuscitation methods, using Resuscitator Annie. Keep abreast of new and changing techniques.

WADING POOL ACTIVITIES

1. The child collects pennies or colored chips from the bottom of the pool.
2. Blowing Bubbles
    a. The child practices blowing bubbles with a straw while walking across the pool.
    b. The child practices blowing bubbles while doing the arm crawl movement.
3. Alligator Races
    a. The child participates in alligator races by crawling in a horizontal position, lifting one hand up at a time off the bottom of the wading pool. (This may also be done in a kneeling position.)
    b. He then tries to lift up both hands while in the horizontal position.
    c. While crawling he adds:
        i.   Kicking
        ii. Blowing bubbles with a straw
        iii. Blowing bubbles with his mouth
4. The child takes a kickboard, and:
    a. Walks it across the pool

    b. Lies on top of it and kicks it across:
        i. Blows bubbles

      ii. Lifts one hand up from the board and then two
          hands from the board
  c. Plays bumping cars by steering his kickboard into
      another's
  d. Pulls another child who is lying on a kickboard

Be aware that the sooner the child learns to use the equipment properly, the better it will be for his development in the aquatics area. Have the child continue to progress.

5. One child walks backward while grasping the hands of a front floating child and pulls him through the water. No kickboards are used. They tell each other to blow bubbles.

The games and stunts suggested in the Red Cross swimming book may be added to create a positive learning atmosphere.

For an eight-lesson unit with a duration of thirty minutes each an instructor may divide the lessons in one of the following ways:

1. By alternating fifteen minutes in the wading pool with fifteen minutes in the shallow area.
2. By conducting the first four sessions in the wading pool and the second four sessions in the shallow area.

If a child cannot pass the designated requirements for specified areas of the pool, his safety with proper supervision must be considered. Flotation devices should be used if necessary, and safety awareness skills designed by the pool's management should be reviewed. After successfully implementing this program, the fundamentals of swimming will have been taught. The aspects of fun will have been incorporated. All that is left is the continued satisfaction of both the child and adult, who is secure in the knowledge that swimming will be safely enjoyed at the appropriate time.

Appendix: Sample Handout

Water Introduction for Infants and Toddlers (W.I.T.)

(Ages six months to two years)

Water Introduction for Preschoolers (W.I.P.)

(Ages three to five)

Instructor's Name:

Instructor's Certification and Background:

Instructor's philosophy or guidelines followed:

    A. Water adjustment program

    B. YMCA guidelines/American Red Cross[8]

    C. Suitable outfit

Instructor's techniques:

    A. Games used to help acquire swimming skills

    B. Emphasis of parental closeness, eye contact, praise, and repetition

Fact Sheet:

    A. Pool temperature

    B. Turnover

    C. Ph/Cl

Purpose of course:

---

[8] Or FAST Swim Program (2019)

A. Development of gross motor skills

B. Development of self-esteem, value, and worth

Date classes start:

(Two sessions a week for four weeks)

Date of completion:

Makeup session:

Bibliography

American Academy of Pediatrics. "Swimming Instruction for Infants." *Pediatrics* (1980)

Ames, Louise Bates, and Joan Ames Chase. *Don't Push Your Pre-schooler*. New York: Harper and Row, 1974

Aquatics Committee of YMCA. *Guidelines for Children Under the Age of Three*. 1982

Bennett, H.J., and Wagner T. Fields. "Acute Hyponatremia and Seizures in an Infant After a Swimming Lesson.: *Pediatrics 72*, (1983) pp. 125-27

Bory, Eva. *Teach Your Child to Swim*. Australia: Tradewinds, 1978.

Brooks, John J., M.D. "The Child Who Nearly Drowns." *Am J Dis Child* 135 (November 1981).

Canadian YMCA, Canadian Red Cross Society and Canadian Pediatric Society of the Canadian Medical Association. Joint policy officially endorsed, 1976.

Caplan, Frank. *The Parenting Advisor*. New York: Anchor Books, 1978.

Caplan, Frank, and Theresa Caplan. *The Power of Play*. Garden City, N.Y.: Anchor Press/Doubleday, 1973.

Cowle, Lucile. *Teaching Your Tot to Swim*. New York: Vantage Press, 1970.

Darpout, H.L., and R.B. Hornick "Clinical Approach to Infectious Diarrhea." *Medicine 52* (1973), pp. 265-70.

Fendler, K., K. Lissak, Maria Romhany, Erzsebet Osz, Rozalia Suzucs, and G.L. Kovacs. "Adaptive Processes in Child Adolescent Swimmers." *Acta Physiologica Academial Scientarium Hungaricae 49*, no. 1. (1971), pp.17-26.

Florey, Linda L. "Studies of Play: Implicating for Growth, Development, and for Clinical Practice." *The American Journal of Occupational Therapy 35*, no. 8 (August 1981).

Flynn, Thomas. "Swimming Instruction for Infants." *Pediatrics*, 1980.

Frank, Barry S., M.D., and Michael Cicero, M.D. "Notes from Readers: More on Swimming Lessons for Infants." *Pediatric Notes*.

Geaney, John H., Attorney at Law. <u>Personal correspondence</u>. Letter, February 14, 1984.

Geda, Mary W., M.D. "Water Babies Intoxication." *Texas Medicine* 78 (December 1982) p. 6.

Gellis, Sydney, M.D. "Giardiasis in an Infant and Toddler Swim Class." *Pediatric Notes 8*, no. 8 (February 1984).

Goldberg, G.N., E.S. Lightner, W. Morgan, et al. "Infantile Water Intoxication After a Swimming Lesson." *Pediatrics* 70 (1982), pp. 599-600.

Ivar, Fandel, M.D., and Eduardo Bancalari, M.D. "Nearing Drowning in Children; Clinical Aspects." *Pediatrics 58*, no.4 (October 1976).

Kellerman, Dr. Johnathan. *Helping the Fearful Child*. New York" W.W. Norton & Co., Inc., 1981.

Koch, Jaroslav. *Total Baby Development*. New York" Wallaby Books, 1976.

Kropp, Robert, and James Schwartz. "Water Intoxication from Swimming." *Journal of Pediatrics* 101 (1982), pp. 947-51.

Lamb, Michael. *Development Trust and Perceived Effectance in Infancy. Advances in Infancy*, vol. 1. Abley Publishing Corporation, 1981.

Levy, Dr. Janice. *The Baby Exercise Book*. New York: Pantheon Books, Random House, 1975.

Losch, Jean. 'Plusses of Early Swim Lessons." *Journal of Physical Education*, 1939.

McGraw, Myrtle. "Swimming Behavior of the Human Infant." *Journal of Physical Education*, 1978.

Makintubee, Sue. "Shigellosis Outbreak Associated with Swimming." *American Journal of Public Health* 77, no. 2, (February 1987), pp. 167-68.

Mann, Barbara. *Infant and Preschool Swimming Direction*. Handout presented to the C.N.C.A., Champaign, IL., November 1976.

Murphy, Margorie. "Pitfalls of Early Swim Lessons." *Journal of Physical Education*, 1978.

Murray, John. *Infaquatics*. New York: William Morrow and Company, 1981.

Myers, Orin. *Swimming & Aquatics Safety*. American National Red Cross, 1981.

Nagle, Margaret. "How Safe are Swimming Classes for Your Baby." *USA Today*, August 6, 1984.

Nelson, Ron. "Straddling the Fence on Infant Swimming." *Journal of Physical Education*, 1978.

Newman, Virginia Hunt. *Teaching an Infant to Swim*. New York: Harcourt Brace Jovanovich Publishers, 1983.

Painter, Genevieve, Ed.D. *Teach Your Baby*. New York: Simon & Schuster, 1971.

Panda, Nirmala. "Pro's and Con's of Infant Swim Classes." *Update* (1981).

Pearn, John H., M.D. "Secondary Drowning in Children." *British Medical Journal* 281 (October 1980), pp. 1101-103.

Pearn, John H., M.d., Joseph Brown III, M.D., Richard Wong, M.D., and Robert Bart, M.D. "Bathtub Drownings: Report of Seven Cases." *Pediatrics* 64 (1979), pp. 68-70.

Peterson, Bradley, M.D. "Morbidity of Childhood Near Drowning." *Pediatrics* 59, no. 3 (March 1977)

Phillips, K.G. "Swimming and Water Intoxication in Infants." *Canadian Medial Association Journal* 136, 11 (June 1, 1987).

Porsolt, R.D., et al. "Forced Swimming in Rats: Hypothermia, Immobility and the Effects of Imipramine." *European J. Phamacol*, no. 4(August 15, 1979), pp. 431-36.

Queena, John, M.D. *A New Life*. New York: Van Nostrand Reinhold Co., 1979, p. 209.

Ruddy, Margaret G., and Marc H. Bornstein. "Cognitive Correlates of Infants' Attention and Maternal Stimulation Over the First Year of Life." *Child Development* 53 (1982), pp. 183-88.

Rylko, Danuta. *Watersafe Your Baby*. Reading, Massachusetts: Addison-Wesley, Co., 1981.

Schieffelin, John. "A New Technique in Water Survival Training." *Pediatric Annual*, no. 11, pp. 45-50.

Scott, Peter H., M.D., and Howard Eiger, M.D. "Immersion Accidents Involving Pails of Water in the Home." *Journal of Pediatrics*, February 1980.

Siegel, Linda S. "Infant Tests as Predictors of Cognitive and Language Development at Two Years." *Child Development* 52 (1981), pp. 545-50.

Spock, Benjamin. *Baby and Child Care*. New York: Pocket Books, 1976.

Sroufe, L. Allan. "Wariness of Strangers and the Study of Infant development." *Child Development* 48 (1977), pp. 731-46.

Sturner, W.Q., F. Spriulli, R.A. Smith, et al. "Accidental Asphyxial Deaths involving Infants and Young Children." *J. Forensic Science* 21 (1976), p. 483.

Thompson, Margaret M., M.D. "Current Growth and Development Knowledge Applied to Infant Preschool Swimming." Paper submitted at the Ramada Inn Conference Center, Champaign, Il., November 1976. (CNCA Preschool Aquatic Program).

Whiting, H.T.A. *Teaching the Persistent Non-Swimmer*. New York: St. Martin's Press, 1970.

Wiener, Harvey. *Total Swimming*. New York: Simon & Schuster, 1980.

About the Author

Linda Bolger is a retired health and physical educator from Eastern High School in Voorhees, NJ and is a staunch swim safety advocate. Linda has earned a Bachelor of Science in Health and Physical Education from West Chester University and a Master's Degree of Health and Physical Education from Glassboro State College, taught swimming lessons for almost fifty years, and operated a successful pool business. As a result of her master's thesis, Linda researched many swimming programs throughout the state of New Jersey. She then authored the book *Dunk Your Doughnuts, Not Your Children* (1988) to motivate instructors to teach swim techniques without forced submersion.

She and her husband, Michael, raised 4 biological children, adopted 4 children, and fostered over one hundred. Through grants, Linda taught swimming to Camden, NJ inner city children and created a life jacket swim program for children with disabilities. Today, Linda (also known as Miss Bubbles) continues her passions and teaches swimming lessons in Northeast Florida. She published the extraordinary swim instruction program FAST (Flotation Aided Swim Training) Swim Program Instructor Guided Learning Manual, which went into second edition in 2019.

Please visit and connect with us!

www.fastswimprogram.com
www.facebook.com/fastswimprogram

www.ingramcontent.com/pod-product-compliance
Lightning Source LLC
Chambersburg PA
CBHW061709250726

48657CB00002B/574